Those Who Can . . . Teach!

Those Who Can . . . Teach!

Celebrating Teachers Who Make a Difference

LORRAINE GLENNON AND MARY MOHLER

Wildcat Canyon Press
A Division of Circulus Publishing Group, Inc.
Berkeley, California

Those Who Can . . . Teach!
Celebrating Teachers Who Make a Difference

Editorial Director: Roy M. Carlisle
Copyeditor: Jean Blomquist
Cover Design: Eleanor Reagh
Interior Design: Gordon Chun Design
Typesetting: Margaret Copeland
Typographic Specifications: Text in New Century Schoolbook; headers in American Typewriter, and Helvetica Black.

Printed in the United States of America

Library of Congress Cataloging-in-Publication Data
Those who can-- teach! : celebrating teachers who make a difference / [compiled by] Lorraine Glennon and Mary Mohler.
   p.   cm.
   ISBN 1-885171-35-8 (pbk.: alk. paper)
1. Teacher-student relationships--United States. 2. Teachers--United States Anecdotes.
I. Glennon, Lorraine. II. Mohler, Mary, 1948- .
LB1033.T56   1999
371.l02'3'0922--dc21   99-39353
                                                           CIP

Distributed to the trade by Publishers Group West
10 9 8 7 6

CONTENTS

DEDICATION

To our parents, Martha and Bob Glennon,
and Albert and Deane Mohler,
who were our first teachers.
And to our children, Claire and Thomas Leavitt,
and Elizabeth, David, and Teddy Trautman,
who bring the lessons home.

FOREWORD

In an era when the issue of education is too often a political football that gets passed back and forth from academics to policy wonks to legislators according to the latest fashion (which seems to change by the week), this resolutely nondoctrinaire book represents an almost radically simple belief: education, at its core, is about the relationship between teachers and students. State-of-the-art computer labs, gyms the size of Montana, course offerings in everything from tantric yoga to the semiotics of post-feminist literary criticism are wonderful features, but all the gyms and computer labs and esoteric curricula in the world cannot compensate for a teacher who fails to get students excited about learning. To be sure, the kind of learning we're talking about thrives in great facilities, but it can also flourish in a one-room schoolhouse.

Happily for this book, great teachers give rise to great stories—poignant, provocative, heartbreaking, hilarious. Like all the former students in this book, we, too, have cherished memories of extraordinary teachers. For years, we've woven tales around the beauty and kindness of Lilah Newman in the second grade, or the erudition and tolerance of Ronald Smith in eighth, and the spellbinding brilliance of Stanley Elkin and Martin Stevens in college. The stories collected here reflect a range of experience as wide as our educational system—from private to public schools, from kindergarten to college, from laid-back methods to deeply traditional—but all underscore the power of an individual educator to make a lasting difference in a student's life. Gathering these stories—a task in which we had the invaluable assistance of our researcher, David M. Fischer—was an education in itself.

It's an education we want to continue. Please share with us your stories of remarkable teachers by writing Teachers, 46 Garfield Place, Brooklyn, NY 11215-1904; or e-mailing GlenLeav@aol.com.

—Lorraine Glennon and Mary Mohler

Editorial Notes

The names of many of the products mentioned in these pages are registered trademarks, belonging to their owners. We fully acknowledge the rights of these owners.

Some individuals' names have been changed and certain characteristics have been disguised to protect privacy.

CHAPTER ONE

Shining Stars and Inspirations

Remember the wonderful scene in *As Good As It Gets* when Jack Nicholson, responding to Helen Hunt's demand for a compliment, says, "You make me want to be a better man"? Certain great teachers have a similar effect on their students. They raise the bar and challenge us to reach for it.

These are the teachers whose deepest lessons sometimes have less to do with math or physics or English than with life; who make us remember our own humanity; who teach us the value of compassion, of having principles, of taking risks for others. Perhaps even more important, they awaken us to our own potential, make us better than we imagined we could be. For them, we gladly work harder than we've ever worked before. These teachers expect nothing less than our personal best—and more often than not, we rise to those expectations. When we fall short, when we lazily insist that our work is good enough, they're always there to remind us, as one of the teachers remembered here puts it, "Not for you, it isn't."

ISAAC MEYER, SUPERHERO

It's a soft, kindly smile that has haunted me for twenty-five years now. It wasn't from some girl with whom I locked eyes across the clichéd crowded room—that would be a pleasant memory, or at least a bittersweet one. No, the smile that chips at my conscience came from my high-school teacher, Isaac Meyer, after I skewered him in public.

I entered my unsung private high school in Queens, New York, in 1971 as a scholarship student and a product of the New York City public education system. To a teen accustomed to a three-ring circus of stiff, bored teachers piloting hordes of listless students in overcrowded classrooms through stale lesson plans, my new school seemed as refreshing as a county fair: human-sized, homey (part of the school was, in fact, a big old house), friendly, with faculty and students who gave a damn. It was like no school I had seen before.

And Mr. Meyer, who taught me geometry and physics in the tenth and eleventh grades, was like no teacher I had known. Just over sixty, he wore his lank silver hair hippie length and sported a shaggy mustache as a countercultural complement. His face was long, with apple cheeks and a powerful jaw as well-defined as a superhero's. He dressed in open-collared shirts and casual pants, and even when he spoke in normal tones, his bass voice penetrated plaster walls.

Mr. Meyer was physically strong, with well-muscled arms. He had one especially impressive trick that he loved to demonstrate: He would order one of us to position a metal-and-wood schoolroom chair upright on a desk. Mr. Meyer then stood a little ways back from the desk, stuck out his arm to full length, grabbed the chair by one of its feet, and hoisted it up while keeping the chair straight and his arm stiff. Not even the buffest athletes in the school could replicate this stunt. Try it yourself, if you think it's easy.

But Mr. Meyer's strengths extended to less visible skills, including his extraordinary prowess as a teacher. In his classes, coming up with the right answer to a math or science problem was almost beside the point; in fact, he frequently provided the answer in advance. What he cared about was how we got there. When solving a geometry proof, for example, we were required to write out not only each step of the solution, but why we chose that particular step. In short, he taught us how to think. In Mr. Meyer's masterly hands, mathematics actually became what the Greeks had intended: a template for looking at life.

And life usually intruded into his classroom, for Mr. Meyer was a man of fiercely liberal social convictions. Some days we didn't talk about math or physics at all but about Nixon or Vietnam or some other fresh outrage riding atop that morning's *New York Times*. To the class's surprise, Mr. Meyer confided that he had been drummed out of the city public school system during the McCarthy era. As far as I know, he never revised his left-wing beliefs, never recanted, never caved in. One weekend he attended his son's wedding; on Monday morning, he told us how he'd been moved to tears when his son, in a toast, compared his dad to Paul Robeson. (Of course, Mr. Meyer then had to explain to us who Paul Robeson was.) If anything, I thought the comparison unjust to Mr. Meyer. Unlike Robeson, he seemed to harbor no bitterness toward those who'd mistreated him. In his retelling of the anecdote, there was more than a hint of self-congratulation. Mr. Meyer was not falsely modest; he knew how good he was. I duly noted the egotism but did not mind it. After all, I agreed with his estimation of himself.

I was undeniably one of the faithful. I stayed after class to chat with him. I did well in his subjects and, at his urging, tutored those who did not. In a word, I worshiped him. And, ultimately, I betrayed him.

For our eleventh-grade English project, the teacher assigned a "creative term paper"—not the standard research-and-write-by-rote exercise but a "unique and expressive" collaborative venture that could take almost any form we chose. Two friends and I decided to create a rock opera—a parody of a current best-selling concept album. In it, we would lampoon the miraculous powers of, and sycophancy inspired by, one of the school's legendary figures. Our English teacher approved the project, but she warned us to proceed carefully. When our source material, *Jesus Christ, Superstar*, became a Broadway musical, there were pickets for days at the theater and condemnations from the pulpit. If our show, *Isaac Meyer, Superstar*, went too far, we were risking, if not damnation, then surely expulsion.

As the lyricist, I reveled in being a wise guy, penning sneering verses about Mr. Meyer, his methods, and his disciples (among whom I'd always counted myself). But why, given the danger and my high regard for the man, did I do it? Teenage bravado, partly—I wanted to see if I could get away with it. For attention, too—I knew this would generate a lot of buzz on the student grapevine. A good grade, of course—I figured I should get an A for chutzpah alone. But also, as I realize now, I was expressing, in a twisted teenage way, my affection and admiration for Mr. Meyer—feelings that would have been unmanly and uncool to express directly. And so, in the manner of adolescents, I ragged on him.

But not too publicly. All three of us were too gutless for that. Anyone who wrote a play for the creative term paper was required to stage it at school, but we decided that our musical had to be cast and rehearsed and make its debut in top-secret circumstances—not an easy task, given the school's size. Our English teacher agreed that we need perform only one scene behind closed doors, in a small rec room where students ordinarily played ping-pong. In the weeks before our opening, there were the inevitable whispered rumors coursing through the school. But our eponymous protagonist seemed oblivious, so I was feeling okay.

Then, hours before the clandestine production was to take place, Mr. Meyer caught me exiting the rec room. Quickly, I shut the door behind me so he wouldn't glimpse our lights, makeshift sets, and musical instruments. He strode up to me, and said "Hey, Itzkowitz!"

"Yes, Mr. Meyer?" I must have had that deer-in-the-headlights look.

He stuck out his arm—the one he used for chair-lifting—put a big hand on my shoulder, and said, "I hear you wrote a parody of me."

I was mute with fear.

Mr. Meyer's eyes fixed on my face, and he tilted his head a little. Then he smiled, widely and sweetly. "It's all right," he said, in the quietest tones I'd ever heard him use, "it's all right."

In a flash, I saw the depths of my betrayal, the whole sorry mess I had made. I'd pilfered his life, mocked his character, just so I could swagger in a moment of high-school limelight. It was a despicable thing to do to a good man. And the good man was good enough to forgive me.

I was dazed, but the brief rec-room performance went well. The term paper as a whole misfired. Judging it controversial but unfunny, our English teacher gave us a thoroughly deserved C+.

C+ or not, that term paper taught me one of the most important lessons I ever learned in sixteen years of school. And it had nothing to do with English, or math, or physics either. It was a lesson about life. And as usual, it was Mr. Meyer who taught it. With a smile and a murmur of absolution, he not only properly shamed me, but he also showed me what true strength was, a strength that lifted something more challenging even than schoolroom chairs: of character, of loyalty, of the bonds of friendship. It was the strength that enabled him not only to survive all that he had endured, but to forgive those of us who recklessly wronged him.—*Harold Itzkowitz*

PRACTICE, PRACTICE, PRACTICE

I wasn't really planning to take calculus until Mr. Escalante found me hiding in Algebra 2 class. Every day he would pass by the classroom and see me there, bored, reading a novel. That just irked him.

Finally he came in and took my book away. To my teacher he said, "How can you let her just sit here and read a book when she's supposed to be paying attention?"

"She's getting the highest grade in the class," the teacher replied.

"Then there's something very wrong here," he said. "She's not being challenged. I'll see to it that she won't be reading books during class." And with that, he made me sign up for his calculus course.

That class was the basis for the 1987 movie *Stand and Deliver*. To say that Jaime Escalante taught the class would be a breathtaking understatement. He lived it with us—before school, in fourth period, through lunch, during sixth period, after school, even on vacations. He knew how the university system worked, and he understood how good calculus looks on your high-school record when you're applying for college and how much confidence it can build. He was there for us, through all those grueling hours, to ensure that we succeeded.

One of the first things Mr. Escalante did in that class was give us the Advanced Placement test so that we could fail it. That may not sound like a recipe for success, but there was something both comforting and challenging in knowing just how much we didn't know. He then took us through the test and systematically taught us everything on it. This technique set limits on our sense of failure and permitted us a concrete sense of accomplishment. By the time we were actually required to take the AP test, it was easy for us, because we had two perspectives: the early one of not even knowing what the problems were asking, let alone having any idea of how to solve them; and the later one of knowing we could get the answer the instant we read through the question because we were so well prepared. Thanks to Mr. Escalante, we were able to see that hard work really does pay off and that it is possible to learn something that initially seems totally overwhelming.

One thing the movie failed to make clear is that most of us were already good students—we were much more serious than those on screen. And though Mr. Escalante was an extraordinary man and an extraordinary teacher, there were others at Garfield High who cared just as much as he did. Mr. Mroscak, the guidance counselor, and Mr. Manyweather, who taught band, are just two of the many who also deserve credit.

In spite of how well I did, and in spite of my gratitude to Mr. Escalante, I must tell you that I have never used calculus since the day I walked out of his class. But then, learning doesn't have a simple quid pro quo. I graduated from the University of Southern California in three years, largely because I took AP and college courses in high school. And having graduated early, I figured I might as well take two more years and get my M.B.A. degree.

The great gift of my education is that it gave me options. These days, I'm a stay-at-home mom with my own human-resources consulting business. I'm doing exactly what I want to be doing, and for me, that's the ultimate definition of success.

I'm teaching my daughter, who's in second grade, the lesson I learned from Mr. Escalante. I tell her, doing math is a lot like playing the piano. It's hard at first, but with practice, you get really good at it.—*Aili Gardea*

ALL THAT JAZZ

At the beginning of fifth grade my mother bought me a saxophone—not because I had displayed some inordinate talent but because she had a crush on Stan Getz. It was my great fortune that a music teacher at my school named Clem de Rosa was starting a band comprised of fifth and sixth graders. Now, I know almost every school in America has a band, but this was something much rarer: a jazz band. Clem was himself a jazz professional—a drummer, though he could play any instrument under the sun—and he brought his high professional standards and expectations to his teaching. His credibility wasn't hurt by the fact that his cool good looks jibed perfectly with the popular image of a jazz musician.

As we got older, he moved up with us, so the nucleus of the band stayed the same all through junior high and high school. By the time we were at Walt Whitman High, in South Huntington, New York, we were recognized as the number one high-school jazz band in America. We appeared on television and gave concerts all over the country.

He used to hold practice at seven in the morning, before classes, or at seven at night, after school. We still took part in sports and all the other extra-curricular stuff kids pursue, but somehow de Rosa got us to make this effort for our music—and he got amazing results. For the first time, I saw that if you really worked at something, no matter how difficult, you could master it. I doubt I appreciated all this at the time, but I took the lesson to heart. It has become an operating principle.

I still don't know how he convinced high school kids to work the way we did, but, ultimately, we did it because we enjoyed it. He made us feel we were talented and very special, because nobody else was doing what we were. And he was right: Imagine a bunch of high-school kids learning to improvise, to play this incredibly sophisticated music! He gradually gave us more and more difficult pieces, but he was always sure we could handle it. And to our astonishment, we could and did.

Before I met de Rosa, I'd always been able to kind of slide through, but with him, those days were over. When we were doing a particularly complicated piece, he'd have a practice session with each of the groups of instruments. He'd get the saxophone section together, and if it was obvious we hadn't prepared, he'd just look at us. Then he'd say quietly, "You'd better have this together the next time," and walk out of the room. Believe me, we had it together the next time.

Yet for all his high expectations and his discipline, he was never punitive. What kept us motivated was the force of his personality and the fact that we were like a family. After all, we'd travel on a bus together for eight hours at a stretch. The experience was something I'd never been exposed to before—having to work really hard, being part of a team, and getting genuine satisfaction from a job well done.

After high school, I went on to college and then to dental school. I never played saxophone "professionally" again, though after dental school, when I finally had some time for myself, the first thing I did was go to a pawnshop and buy a used sax. To the consternation of my neighbors, I'm sure, I sometimes take it out in the evenings and play, just for the pleasure of it.

About eight months ago, I got a call from de Rosa, whom I hadn't seen since 1964. He told me that he'd compiled a CD of the music our band had made—we used to cut a record every year—and that he'd been presenting it at educational forums. As one of the pioneers in jazz education, he's still very active in teaching. So after more than thirty years, we got together to listen to the old cuts. He'd been in touch with most of the other band members; nearly all of them are successful, and many are professional musicians. Clem is currently the musical director of the Benny Goodman Orchestra, and when he tours, he often uses musicians who played in his high school bands all those years ago.

There are many teachers you like, but few you can wholeheartedly respect. Clem was one of those, and his lessons have stayed with me. Giving 100 percent to something you believe in and having faith that difficult goals can be achieved—this, for me, is Clem de Rosa's legacy.
—*David Levine*

BREATHING LESSONS

Ms. Grasby, my new fifth-form sociology teacher, was the first "Ms." I ever met. She wore bright, embroidered peasant skirts and shiny cowboy boots. She strode around the classroom, gesticulating with her long-fingered hands. I watched, completely taken aback by the enthusiasm and the anger with which she seemed to love life.

It was 1976. I was fifteen and bored beyond words by the tiny East Yorkshire town in which I grew up and the small-minded, grim-faced people there who faced the future with bleak resignation, talking happily only of the past.

I had taken sociology for no other reason than that, due to a scheduling conflict, it meant I could escape another year of religious education. But on that first day when Ms. Grasby walked into the classroom, wafting her patchouli scent and eager smile over us all, I found myself enthralled.

At first, I liked her merely because she was so different in a place of such barren homogeneity—mid-thirties, unmarried, unconventionally dressed, and shamelessly using that strange title—that even her colleagues took pleasure in hissing at her, faces set in nasty, leering smiles. But after a short time, I began to like her because she genuinely liked us; she never once used humiliation as a punishment or dismissed us with a sarcastic comment. Her lessons were well prepared and orderly, but she also encouraged lively, even heated, discussions. And she asked us questions that no one had posed before: What did we think of the class system? Should Britain abolish the monarchy? Was education a privilege or a right? In all my other classes, textbooks were treated like holy writ, unquestionably infallible. Ms. Grasby committed the revolutionary act of asking us to voice our own opinions. If I merely copied down complete sentences or paragraphs—a technique that had invariably earned me A's in other teachers' classes—she voiced such profound disappointment that it became unbearable to let her down.

What I learned from Ms. Grasby changed my life. She introduced the concept of sexism, and I discovered a vocabulary for all the things that had happened to me as a girl but that until that moment I had been unable to name. When she asked why we used words like "poufter," "homo," and "lezzie" as insults, I felt the first small crack of light fall upon the darkness I had dreaded in myself for so long. And when she nodded at our exasperation at school rules that required us to wear uncomfortable and ugly uniforms, to leap to attention when the headmaster entered a classroom, and to recite prayers we did not believe in, we felt perhaps there was one adult who could empathize with the anger and powerlessness of youth.

She saw in me what I had not recognized: a hunger for something better. She taught me that I had to work for it but that I deserved it. She spent hours helping me with the university and grant applications that baffled me and my parents. And when, as I was about to take exams, I felt myself succumbing to panic, she took me by the shoulders, looked into my eyes, and firmly instructed me to "just breathe." That simple instruction got me through the exam—and so many things since then.—*Elaine Beale*

THE POWER OF SILENCE

I met Vicky Jenkins the summer of my freshman year at boarding school, when on a whim, I signed up for rowing. As we sloshed up and down the Connecticut River in our tree-trunk-thick wooden boats, Vicky trolled behind in a school launch. We were horrendous rowers, unbalanced and awkward. Rather than point out our flaws, Vicky simply let the creaking of the boat and the sloppy slapping of the blades echo in our ears. Occasionally, we'd hear an insightful observation or a word of encouragement from the launch before the wind carried it away. We left determined to do better the next day.

We were too young and fidgety to know that only by relaxing and experiencing each stroke individually would we find the balance and rhythm we sought. Caught up in my freshman fervor, I barely registered Vicky's presence in the launch. All I knew was that she coached girls' varsity crew in the spring, taught math, and owned energetic dogs who bounded out of her cream-yellow Chevy Blazer each day, eager, like us, to play in the river.

Over the next three years, Vicky emerged from the chaos of my life to become a figure of powerful and enduring significance. When I reflect on those years, I tend to remember first the bustle and stir, the activity that never let up, the clamor of each day. But memories of the river are couched in silence. A certain peace pervaded our glorified garage of a boathouse. The day, filled with instructions and directions, would end with the calm of Vicky's practice, where instruction always came second to self-direction.

Quite simply, Vicky revealed to me that action was sometimes better than words, and that silence could prove more powerful than the endless hyperconscious chatter we too often engage in.

In a letter she sent me the summer before my senior year, when I worked as a camp athletic director with young girls, Vicky wrote:

I personally feel that too many girls—and women—spend more time wondering how others will perceive them than doing what comes naturally. One of the exceptions to this is girls who are involved in sports. Participation in athletics develops the individual, making her content with herself, or at least able to make decisions about what would make her happier. The best way to get the tentative girls going is to let them watch you have fun (and, yes,

they will watch your every move) and then encourage them, no mat-
ter how terrible or awkward they may be.

I understood only a part of her wisdom, but I continued to struggle
with defining myself apart from expectation and perception.

Just as Vicky watched my progress from the launch, I watched her
too. Although dynamic and engaged, she was never didactic or heavy-
handed. In her I saw a glimpse of what I hoped to become—a woman
who could be at once blunt and eloquent, assertive and gracious, defiant
and delightful. I never imagined that she was flawless, but I saw that
she had somehow achieved in her life the balance we strove for while
rowing. The various parts of her life, while individually not perfect, had
a coherence, solidity, and beauty I could not help admiring. Her presence and steadfast guidance inspired me to be a little stronger, a little
more confident, than I thought I could be.

While splashing up and down the Connecticut so many years ago, I
thought I would become a journalist, or perhaps an artist. Much to my
own surprise, I am a teacher. At times, as I stand before my English
classes, hoping to convey some of Vicky's calm brilliance, I think I hear
the distant purr of a launch cutting through the water, with a slender
and striking figure on board. She looks at me with quiet confidence, daring me, as always, to amaze myself.—*Claire Leheny*

REQUIEM FOR A MAESTRO

On the first day of class Dr. Magis told us, "After having studied litera-ture for years, with two doctorates in the field, and having written two long academic books on literature, I realized that I didn't know how to read. So in this seminar we are going to try to begin to learn how to read—that is, read a text profoundly and carefully."

There were only six of us in his Seminar on the Reading of Contemporary Texts. We met on Tuesdays at his small, round dining-room table. His collection of indigenous ceremonial masks stared down at us, seeming to listen as we discussed poems or stories by Leopoldo Lugones, Horacio Quiroga, Octavio Paz, Ernesto Cardenal, Julio Cortázar, and Jorge Luis Borges.

Dr. Magis must have been in his late fifties, though because he was stooped and bald, he appeared older. He encouraged us to speak our minds and feelings about the texts we discussed "con toda confianza"— in trust and sincerity. I was inspired and gratified by his vast patience with my ignorance.

Subtly and without much ado, he inspired a lust for reading. The assignment for each week was to read—profoundly and carefully—a group of poems or stories. Other supportive texts—criticism, commentary, or theory—were suggested but not obligatory. Never did he take for granted that we had previously read a particular book, critic, or author. It was as though we were setting out on an expedition with him as our guide.

For me, his class was a tonic. I had become weary of what seemed to me an overly-scientific approach to literature—a heavy concentration on methodology and theories of analysis. With Dr. Magis, I felt like a weary traveler finding rest.

Halfway through the two-hour session, his housekeeper would serve tea, and we would wrap up our discussion of the text at hand. That's when our conversation would deepen and become both more personal and more universal—but always somehow related to our reading. After all, what could be more personal and more universal than literature? He took it out of the laboratory and put it back into human hands. I always walked away from there with an eagerness to read, study, write, live, and love.

After six or eight weeks of this exhilarating routine, I arrived to find the lobby of his building unusually quiet. Seeing another student approaching, I waited for her. We took the elevator three floors up and knocked at Apartment 303. The housekeeper motioned us inside.

"I have bad news for you," she said, gazing at the floor instead of our faces. "The maestro was taken to the hospital on Friday. Yesterday he asked for a priest to give him last rites; this morning he had another heart attack." She turned away and sobbed.

The masks on the wall above the little table where we had held our sessions stared down with lifeless eyes, now no more than painted wood and clay. The books lining the living room walls from floor to ceiling seemed old and shabby. I felt lost in a forest but grateful I had wandered there, following the slow, uneven lead of my guide, Maestro Magis.

—*James Miller Robinson*

IGNORANT ROCK

Five guys were shuffling around outside the doorway to Mr. Rohdes's Earth Science class. I hung quietly behind them, the lone girl among the school's most notorious screw-ups, trying to decide whether to blow off this class, when Mr. Rohdes stepped into the hall. He was a slight man who looked like a magnet for bullies. "Hey, come on in," he said, his right hand making a sweeping gesture. "Your desks await you."

"Nah," said Hager. "My old man beat my brains out long ago."

"Then you must be here to admire my profile," said Mr. Rohdes. Turning his head sideways, he displayed his jutting lower jaw, which he declared one of the geologic wonders of the world. The boys snickered. Hager said, "I just came by to see how dumb your joke was today."

"Okay, you asked for it." Grabbing the chalk, Mr. Rohdes printed in neat white letters: "What kind of music does a stale biscuit remind you of?" He paused for a moment and then wrote: "Rock 'n' Roll." Everyone groaned. Hager said, "Man, you're something else."

Yes, Mr. Rohdes was different. Some teachers at our crowded urban high school made it clear they thought we were losers. Others acted as if they were serving hard time. Not Mr. Rohdes.

I watched the guys head off down the hall. When I looked back into the classroom, Mr. Rohdes was waving me in. "Please, join us." Suddenly feeling exposed, I hurried in and found an empty desk, just as Mr. Rohdes was holding up an object for the class to see. "This is an ignorant rock." Someone called out, "How ignorant?"

"Stone ignorant," Mr. Rohdes said, and the class laughed. "Come on, what's it really?" a student asked. On the blackboard, Mr. Rohdes wrote, "Igneous rock." Turning back to us, he said, "This rock was once molten liquid because it was in a place hotter than hell." He paused. "And that place was right here at the core of our earth."

I only half listened to the lecture. I couldn't get my mind off my father. I'd seen him outside church on Sunday with his wife. There he'd stood, smiling and shaking hands with the priest. But the night before he'd been on the phone to my mother, begging her to meet him. Promising to leave his wife for her.

The bell sounded. While the other kids stormed out, I drifted to the front of the room to look at the rock. "You've missed a lot of school," Mr. Rohdes said. Startled, I said, "So? I'm just an ignorant rock."

"Rocks are strong too," he said. "I'd be happy to help you catch up, if you'd like."

For the rest of the week, I skipped school.

When I returned to class, Mr. Rohdes was giving a quiz. I stared at the questions and knew I had no hope. I was sixteen now; I might as well drop out. My mother had gotten straight A's and where had it gotten her? Anyway, the dean of students had just told me I had no future.

"Can I speak to you a moment?" Mr. Rohdes whispered. I stared at his jutting jaw and clenched my fist. But then a weird thing happened. His hand touched my shoulder, and I wanted to cry instead.

"Are you okay?"

I shook my head.

"Why don't you go into my office and sit quietly for a while?"

All over his office, rocks perched precariously on stacks of books and papers. Under a window an old sofa basked in the spring sunshine. I collapsed on it and closed my eyes.

After a while Mr. Rohdes came in. He put the quizzes on his desk. "I thought I'd just give you an A," he said. "To help you out."

"I don't want you to give me an A," I retorted.

"I didn't think you would," he said. "You're too smart. I looked up your grades."

"Your eyesight bad?"

"No, but I saw your IQ." He came over to the sofa and sat down. "You can get your own A's. In fact, I bet if we went over the chapter right now, you'd ace the quiz."

He picked up an odd-shaped object that sat on the windowsill and handed it to me. "This is a quartz crystal."

Its base looked like broken shards of glass, but out of it arose clear, smooth-sided prisms. "Does it come from the stars?" I asked.

"No," he responded, "from common materials right here on earth. But look what they've made of themselves."

I aced the quiz, just as Mr. Rohdes had predicted. And over the next year I set about making something of myself. That spring of 1965, Mr. Rohdes showed me how and why.—*Meredythe Crawford*

WHEN "GOOD ENOUGH" ISN'T

Her name was Mary Lou Wallace, and the first thing I noticed was her copper-colored hair. She would have called it brown. She was what was known, in that part of the country at that time, as a "plain-spoken woman." Her manner was direct, her principles solid. Her judgments were as uncompromising as they were well-considered. She was so much the epitome of a no-nonsense English teacher that it would be decades before I realized that, when I knew her, she was also very young.

It was 1965, and I was in eighth grade at Bethel Junior High School in Bethel, Connecticut. Years later—when Bethel had become one of the hottest suburbs in Fairfield County—the school would become almost famous as the place where Meg Ryan was almost elected homecoming queen. In my day, however, it was a backwater where nobody ever seemed to do anything important when they grew up.

I'm not sure what was wrong with me that year. I had decided to be a writer when I was six. I had a bookcase full of Hemingway novels and daily fantasies of living in Paris. For some reason, though, it had all stalled somewhere inside my head. I woke up every day in a sea of misery, painfully aware of the fact that I had suddenly become "weird," out of it, not part of the group. Even the two girls who were ostensibly my friends were exasperated with me. They didn't like the books I read. They were embarrassed by the music I listened to. They thought my dreams of college were just plain nuts. "Why would anybody want to go to college," one of them said, "except for the parties?"

And so, because I am gregarious, maybe because I'm a coward, I was trying desperately to fit in. I giggled a lot. I loudly proclaimed that I hated school. I pretended not to do well and sometimes didn't have to pretend: I stopped studying, wouldn't read, and goofed off so that my grades would not be the sort that would make people laugh at me.

The one place I didn't goof off was in Miss Wallace's class—partly because I didn't want to and partly because I couldn't. Anybody, even a child, who writes every day for six years will write better than those who haven't. My essays came back with good grades and sometimes terrifying comments in the margins. "You could do this for a living if you wanted to," one of them said. I remember leaving class and walking straight to a big trash bin near the gym, to rip that essay to shreds and throw it out. I was scared to death that somebody important—Janie or Debbie, Kathy or Sue—would see it.

In the middle of this mess, my father decided that I ought to go to private school. I took the suggestion as if it were a sentence to drink hemlock. A private school? All girls? Uniforms? He had to be kidding.

At the end of the year, though, I was stuck. Miss Wallace stood in front of our class and asked anyone who'd be attending a different school the following year to fill out a card for the office. I still hadn't agreed to go, but I knew I had to get the card anyway, just in case.

At the end of the period, I started to leave the room, and Miss Wallace stopped me.

"Are you moving?" she asked me.

"No," I said. "My father wants to send me away to school."

"And . . .?"

I launched into my whining complaint—all girls, no boys, it would be snobbish, there would be uniforms, I didn't want to go to school with a lot of strangers. She let me go on for quite a while. Then she said, "Don't be ridiculous."

"I'm not being ridiculous," I told her. "It's how I feel."

"We can't possibly give you what a first-class private school could. We don't have the resources. You could do something significant with your life if you were challenged enough to work to capacity."

"But I am being challenged," I said. "I'm fine." And then I dug into my notebook and came out with the latest of my English essays, graded A+. "Look—I'm doing great. This is great."

Mary Lou Wallace looked me up and down and said, "Not for you, it isn't."

I don't know why that particular comment should have gotten through to me when nothing else could, but it did. The shift within my brain was almost physical. The person staring back at me in my metaphorical mirror had been suddenly transformed. Not for you, it isn't. Not for me, because I had other options. Not for me, because all the qualities that I had been so ashamed of in myself were the ones I should have been proud of.

I didn't go to private school that next year. I waited until tenth grade, when I was fifteen and more ready to make the move. What I did start doing was carrying my books again, out in the open. And finishing my schoolwork. And holding on to my A+ papers instead of burying them in the trash.

I haven't seen Miss Wallace in more than thirty years, but her voice still lives inside my head. I have become a mystery novelist, and on those late nights when I have written the latest chapter of my latest book fourteen times and I'm bone-tired and my conscious mind is saying, "You've done everything you can do—it's good enough," Miss Wallace sits on my shoulder saying, "Not for you, it isn't."—*Jane Haddam*

THE DROPPINGS OF A GREAT MIND

"Questions, scholars."

Even now, filtered through the haze of memory, I hear that voice. Deep, resonant, a tad ironic. This was how Jim Lewis began history class each morning at Wayzata High School in Plymouth, Minnesota.

He'd walk in just as the bell sounded—portly, bearded, a commanding presence. In lieu of a desk, he sat in a black leather rocker, front and center in the wide, shallow room. A moment of quiet, as he surveyed us with an omniscient air. Severe, square glasses framed his tiny, intense, coal-black eyes (were I less reverent, I'd call them beady). He swiveled subtly in that easy chair, fingered his cigar cutter absently, and we'd have at it.

We asked questions; he answered them. That's all. No lectures. No pop quizzes. He expected us to do the (extensive) reading each night and come prepared to discuss. And God help us if we didn't have questions. He told us early on, in a matter-of-fact tone that managed to sound like the direst threat, "If you have nothing to ask me, then I begin to ask you. And trust me, you don't want me asking the questions."

Until this point, I had taken good grades for granted and coasted to A's with minimal effort. Not with Mr. Lewis. Unrelenting in his insistence that we use our brains, he dared us to think, to analyze, to question. We—who used to believe that plagiarizing a few decrepit books from the school library would suffice—now studied college-level textbooks, struggled through multiple-essay tests.

For three years—tenth through twelfth grades—a core group of us stayed with him, through the Reconstruction and Teapot Dome, from Martin Luther to the Treaty of Versailles. Senior year, one class was devoted entirely to Jacob Bronowski's *The Ascent of Man*, no less than a scientific and intellectual history of civilization. Imagine a room of seventeen-year-olds debating the religious implications of Copernican astronomy, the philosophical connection between music and calculus. We were too young and too inexperienced to realize how blessed we were—even though other faculty members occasionally reminded us. One day, the English teacher in the adjacent classroom, Steve Root, poked his head in to ask Mr. Lewis a question. As he was leaving, Mr. Root looked at us and said, "Pay attention, kids. You are listening to the droppings of a great mind." Naturally, we all tittered, but now I know Mr. Root was right.

Yes, Mr. Lewis's high standards terrified me; I dreaded not being good enough. But I came back for more, knowing he—and eventually I—would settle for nothing less. Looking back, I am convinced there was nothing he didn't know. But in time, I saw the man behind the stern image. The piercing eyes that could cow even the most boorish adolescent could also twinkle with devilish mirth. Though he often demurred, "I'm not being facetious!" he did, in fact, nurse a pungent wit.

Still, there was the temptation to skate. I was a foolish teenager, after all, my attention diverted by boys, bad hair days, and music videos. One sloppy night, I scribbled a slapdash extra-credit report on *The Catcher in the Rye*, a book I had read five times already. It was a gamble, but misplaced hubris convinced me it was enough to get by.

The report came back with one simple comment: "Just think how much better this would have been if you had made a sincere effort." My stomach still lurches at the memory. I got the extra credit but couldn't meet his gaze for weeks. Conversely, nothing has ever pleased me more than the brief message tacked onto the bottom of the last paper I wrote for him: "It has been a pleasure teaching you."

My friend Robin, a fellow Lewis survivor, says it best: "He made every one of us take responsibility for our own education." At seventeen, of course, I was utterly unaware of the magnitude of that gift.

I'd like to say that knowing him changed the course of my life—that I picked up his gauntlet and drove myself to excel. But life rarely follows such a tidy script. The disheartening truth is, most people don't expect excellence, much less demand it. And it's hard to stay motivated in a world that rejoices at mere competence. Life becomes an exercise in endurance, where success means getting by, even as it saps your soul.

As for me, the frustrated author, I have vowed this: When I write my first book, I will dedicate it to Jim Lewis. No one has ever challenged me so completely. And if it does come to pass, it will be because I finally lived up to the potential that, long ago, a wise and patient man saw in a bright but insecure young girl.—*Kelly Regan*

CHAPTER TWO

Mentors, Masters, and Muses

Think of Aristotle at the feet of Plato; Alexander at the feet of Aristotle. This notion of apprenticeship, of a protégé absorbing the craft and wisdom of a master, is one of the oldest and noblest traditions in education. These educators are role models in the deepest, truest sense of that much-abused term: they are the men and women we want to emulate.

It is notable that in one of the stories included in this chapter, a photograph of the mentor watches over the former student as she pursues her chosen profession. For many of us, that picture is metaphorical but no less real: an image we keep in our minds or a voice that whispers in our ear as we see patients, as we write, as we teach.

Sometimes we set out to find a mentor, but just as often, our mentors acquire us. Intent on becoming a doctor, we meet a master and feel suddenly compelled to study not biochemistry but Keats; even more unsettling, perhaps we were content to simply get by, to settle, with no ambition greater than to make a living—when an extraordinary teacher ignites in us a desire to become something more. And when such a teacher opens a door, we have no choice but to walk through it.

A FRIENDSHIP, STILL UNFADED

I come from sturdy Alabama farming stock, from pecan orchards and peanut fields. By rights my favorite flower ought to be something straightforward and simple, something that thrives in red clay and drought—zinnias, maybe, or marigolds or black-eyed Susans. It's true I've always been fond of these ordinary yard flowers, plants that drop their own seeds and come back, summer after hazy summer, without any effort on the gardener's part. I've come to think of these plain blossoms, which have no real fragrance, as the floral objective correlative of myself. But despite my appreciation for them, they aren't the ones I love best. My favorite flower is not a sturdy State Fair zinnia. My favorite flower is a fragile, milky white, heavenly scented gardenia.

I was in high school before I encountered a gardenia bloom for the first time. It was floating in a glass bowl on my favorite teacher's desk, and when I walked in a little early that morning, her whole classroom was filled with its scent. For a moment I forgot the chalk dust and the cinderblock walls and the frantic fervor of movement out in the hall. For a moment I stood still and breathed in that heady, perfect fragrance. It was the divine sort of scent that ought to accompany an apparition of the Virgin Mary or the opening of heaven's gates before a loving and generous soul.

As I stood there in the doorway, lifting my nose again and again and sniffing like some sort of animal whose very life depends upon smells carried in the air, my teacher looked up from her desk and smiled. "The blooms last only a day," she said, "so I always cut them and bring them along. I can't bear to let the fragrance go to waste in an empty house."

To me the scent of a gardenia is invariably a reminder of that teacher, Ann West Granberry, who taught me both British poetry and the necessity of flowers. But because I loved her, and because she was very ill during the last year she taught me—dying, at thirty-seven, the summer after I graduated—the bloom of a gardenia is also a reminder of just how brief our time on earth can be.

For three years, Ann Granberry was the adult I needed most besides my parents. Because she was both my teacher and an advisor to the school newspaper I edited, I spent more than two hours a day in her company. But I was not the only student who loved her, and it was never easy to find a moment for private conversation. I used to stand outside the school, in a grove of trees between the parking lot and the gym fields, and wait for her to leave the building. For a few moments in the failing light, I could have her all to myself.

"Margaret, are you grieving over Goldengrove unleaving?" she would joke in autumn, quoting Hopkins when she saw me standing there among the red dogwoods and the yet low maples beside the teachers' parking lot. I always laughed, to prove I got the joke. I was sixteen. I never imagined the grieving would begin so soon.

In the late spring of my junior year, Mrs. Granberry discovered a lump under her left arm. By the time she returned to teach in the fall, she was gravely ill. My classmates and I knew she was dying; for her part, despite unwavering hope, Mrs. Granberry understood how poor were her odds. She talked to us honestly, in a way that adults rarely talk to teenagers, not only about love and art and death—those abstractions that come up again and again in poetry—but also about her own feelings that dark year.

"I'm going to look a little different when I come to class tomorrow," she told us one morning, her voice quavering, the fingers of one hand twining nervously through what had been her thick brown hair. "I had to get a wig. It'll look odd, I'm sure, and I wanted to warn you so . . . ."

Her eyes suddenly glistened, and she didn't go on.

There were other times when a note of fear would creep into Mrs. Granberry's voice. She would clear her throat or wince or put her head into her hands for a moment, and we would look around at each other, terrified. It didn't happen often, but it happened, and when it did, not one of us knew what to say. We were still kids, still felt like kids, but abruptly our roles had been reversed; suddenly it was our job to offer comfort, to pat her on the shoulder, to murmur awkwardly that everything was going to be all right. Half the time we would sit wordless at our desks and look miserably at our folded hands.

That year I spent less time doing my homework than writing Mrs. Granberry letters, night after night, trying to put into words what she meant to me, trying to give her courage to go on. I kept drafts of those letters, only a few of which I ever delivered, and reading them now is a source of both embarrassment and wonder—at my juvenile philosophy, at my awkward words, at my inexpressible love. Across the years I become the girl I was, struggling to understand what as a grown woman I still can't accept: people die no matter how much you love them.

Mrs. Granberry's memorial service was one of my life's surreal events. It was a glorious full-summer morning, and the church was packed. As a sign of his faith in her ultimate resurrection, her deeply religious husband had dressed himself and both their little boys entirely in white, and the organist played, to my shock, Beethoven's *Ode to Joy*. I didn't sing along. I stared around me at the immobile, stained-glass windows, at the sprays of bloodless, snow-white flowers whose fragrance was too weak to fill that cavernous church, and I tried to imagine what my world would be like without her in it.

Ann Granberry has been dead now half my life, but in fact my world has never lacked her presence. I spent twelve years teaching teenagers the same poems she taught me. I keep her picture on my desk. And today, my gardenia bush bloomed in its pot on the back-door steps. I caught its scent early this morning even before I saw the single creamy flower opened among the glossy green leaves. As always, it seemed to me a scene fit for angels.

Suddenly, standing very still, I thought of Tennyson and a poem Ann Granberry taught me long, long ago:

> *Far off thou art but ever nigh;*
> *I have thee still, and I rejoice;*
> *I prosper, circled with thy voice;*
> *I shall not lose thee though I die*

> —Margaret Renkl

THE NEW MATH

My seventh-grade math class got off to a disastrous start. The short, tidy woman who taught it delivered her introductory remarks in a high, nasal voice. "Math is not fun," she warned. "It's a system, and you must learn it systematically. You start with the building block of addition, then you pile on the building blocks of subtraction, multiplication, and division. I will drill you on these building blocks, then move on to algebra, geometry, and trigonometry. Then I will drill you on those."

All I could think was "Get me out of here."

Neither the times—it was 1967—nor my urban bohemian family life had prepared me for this teacher's plodding approach. Like most of my fellow students at my all-girls' junior high, I'd never liked math much anyway. If I stayed in this class, I would surely grow to despise it.

A friend passed on the rumor that the other seventh-grade math teacher, Mr. Nadel, was "nice." On that basis, I begged my advisor to transfer me to his class.

I got lucky: Mr. Mark Nadel *was* nice—a truly kind and gentle man. More important, though, he was a dedicated teacher. Years before anybody else was talking about girls and math anxiety, Mr. Nadel was patiently breaking down our resistance and fear, bit by bit, day by day. He reveled in the intellectually juicy high points of math—negative numbers, elementary logic, and various bases other than 10—and invited us to do the same.

I still remember the thrill of standing up in front of the class after Mr. Nadel asked me to prove that $0.\overline{9}$ (0.999. . . repeating infinitely) actually equals 1. My mother happened to be visiting the class that day. The closest either she or my father had ever come to a mathematical activity was listening to the wonderful songwriter and math professor Tom Lehrer's then-current song "New Math"—and, in truth, they didn't really get the lyrics. So, even if they had been inclined to help me with homework, my parents could never have helped with my math. This was a blessing, as it turned out, because it allowed me to experience the rarefied joy at the heart of so many specialized academic, scientific, and artistic endeavors: understanding and caring deeply about something that most other people don't even know exists.

Mr. Nadel opened a big mental door for me, one that I'm convinced would otherwise have remained shut. Buoyed by my sudden interest in math, I shifted direction, eventually majoring in biology in college and taking graduate courses in biochemistry.

In the parlance of the times, Mr. Nadel "turned me on" to math. But thankfully, unlike many of our faculty, he never tried to be hip. Nor did he tend toward the dramatic, even narcissistic, personality of most of my other favorite teachers—flamboyant, larger-than-life types who taught the world according to them. Mr. Nadel did not teach the world according to Mark Nadel. He taught math. And, ironically, by revealing its joys, he drew me into the subject deeply enough to give me the motivation to slog through the dreaded drills that had propelled me into his classroom in the first place.—*Rebecca Hughes*

A WILLOW IN THE WIND

I attended the Buckingham School, a small all-girls' day school in Cambridge, Massachusetts, where many students' parents were professors at nearby Harvard and MIT. The Buckingham curriculum was excellent, but traditional to the core: Western history, English literature, French, Latin. Then, in 1957, one of the teachers, Elizabeth Stowe, convinced Buckingham's headmistress to initiate a tenth-grade class in Chinese history. Today, such courses are commonplace, but forty years ago, this was a daring educational experiment. To my knowledge, no other secondary school in New England, and most likely America, offered anything remotely like it.

Indeed, in the early days of the class, Mrs. Stowe was still learning the material herself. But what she lacked in knowledge, she more than made up for in enthusiasm—both for her subject and for the challenge of tackling and teaching something new. By the time I enrolled in Chinese history, in autumn 1959, she was no longer a novice, but her enthusiasm was as contagious as ever.

On the surface, Mrs. Stowe was prim and old-fashioned. Her way of calling the class to order was to say, "Ladies, I didn't invite you all to chatter!" She dressed in drab colors, wore no makeup, and would send any girl who dared put on lipstick to the bathroom to wash it off. She was no intellectual, especially compared to other teachers in the school—a group so extraordinary that in eight years at Harvard, I encountered only two professors who rivaled their gifts—and she struggled with spelling. But when she stood in front of a classroom, those shortcomings melted away.

On the first day of our tenth-grade class, Mrs. Stowe read aloud a poem from the Chou Dynasty (1112 B.C. – 249 B.C.):

My lord is full of delight.
In his left hand he holds a flute.

With his right he summons me to play with him.
Oh, what sweet joy!

My lord is full of blessing.
In his left hand he holds dancing plumes.
With his right he summons me to dance with him.
Oh, what sweet joy!

Mrs. Stowe was clearly captivated by this romantic voice from ancient China, and she wanted us to share her sense of enchantment.

Throughout the months that followed, Mrs. Stowe emphasized not only China's political and military past (a standard approach to teaching history in 1959), but its literature and art as well (a much more imaginative method). So along with the dates of the Tang Dynasty, which I still remember, I also acquired a passion for Chinese culture, which I still treasure.

I went on to Harvard, where I studied international affairs. But I never strayed far from China. I took three years of Chinese to satisfy the Ph.D. requirement for a second foreign language. I wrote both my undergraduate and Ph.D. theses on modern China. Unfortunately, the Cultural Revolution, which Mao Zedong unleashed in 1966 to purge the Chinese Communist Party of "enemies," prevented me from visiting the land I had spent so much time trying to understand.

Eventually I grew tired of studying a country that I couldn't see for myself, so I moved to Washington and pursued a mainstream career in foreign affairs. But I never lost interest in East Asia, and I never stopped believing that truly understanding a country requires knowing its history and culture. In the 1980s, I developed an interest in Japan and wrote a book on U.S.-Japan relations from that perspective.

When I finally visited China in 1998—to present papers on U.S.-China-Japan relations and the U.S. model of a market economy system—my hosts were impressed with my obvious respect for their country's history and culture. After one meeting, a Chinese official approached me with shining eyes and thanked me for quoting the great eighth-century poet Li Po: "The peach blossom follows the moving water." It was Mrs. Stowe who had introduced me to Li Po.

Over the mantelpiece in my Washington home hangs a nineteenth-century scroll featuring a single Chinese character meaning "willow." A willow tree symbolizes someone who bends in a storm rather than remaining stiff and being blown over by the wind. To me, it also represents someone capable of bending with the winds of change and growing in unusual directions. Whenever I look at it, I'm reminded of that visionary teacher of four decades ago.—*Ellen L. Frost*

A MIRACLE OF RARE DEVICE

On the first day of Mr. Wilkerson's sixth-grade class, we discussed what we did over the summer. I had gone to India, where my family is from, so I talked about my trip. Mr. Wilkerson started asking me where I'd gone, what I'd liked about it, when my parents had come here—questions no one else had ever asked before. Eastern North Carolina in the 1970s was not the most open-minded place. I constantly heard remarks like, "Oh, you come from the place where cows walk around the street." But I never heard them in Mr. Wilkerson's class. He wanted to learn about my background, and he wanted to make us all feel comfortable with one another.

At that time, classes were typically separated into three tracks, according to how smart everyone was. It was a terrible system that managed to humiliate everyone. But Mr. Wilkerson simply ignored it. In his class, we were all together. We were a community, and the world was just a bigger version of that community. He assigned us a global project in which each student had to be partnered with a country. I drew Syria, so for four months I combed books and newspapers, immersing myself in Syrian culture, people, and religions.

He loved projects, and he used them to turn kids on to science. He dug up an old chicken incubator, and we incubated eggs, opening one up every three days to chart the growth of the chicken. We would groan and say, "This is really gross. I can't believe you're making us do this!" But it was fascinating. When we were studying the parts of an eye, he brought in cows' eyes, which we dissected to examine the cornea and the iris. Kids in other classes were always jealous of the yucky things Mr. Wilkerson had us doing.

When we reenacted the ancient Olympics, we had to go to the library and research what the original games were like. But Mr. Wilkerson made sure we knew what to do. He had us meet him in groups of four at the Greenville Public Library on a Saturday. There, for an entire day, he showed us how to use primary resources.

He constantly sought new ways to expand our world, get us intellectually excited, and keep us curious once we left his classroom. Whenever I see my old school chums, we always end up talking about Rick Wilkerson's class. We all remember the time he blew up at us. For our global project, we had written letters to ambassadors. The day after we turned them in, he walked into class and threw them back on our desks, shouting, "There are spelling mistakes! I didn't teach you to write this way!"

But that episode stands out because he was a gentle soul who did not get upset easily. And it was never over the big mistakes. Those he saw as learning opportunities. It was the little things, the spelling errors that should have been caught, that really annoyed him.

I eventually went to Duke University for my master's in public policy, intending to go to medical school. But when my mentor asked me what I would do if I could do whatever I wanted, I told him that I'd write children's books and start a fund for child literacy programs.

I am now the Executive Director of the Global Fund for Children, which promotes the human rights of children. We publish multicultural children's books and we give grants to community-based educational projects through the Xanadu Arts Education Project. For the Xanadu Project, we partner with public school teachers of art, English, and social studies, who put teams of students together to imagine their ideal place to live, which they call Xanadu.

There's a marvelous line in Samuel Taylor Coleridge's dream poem, "Kubla Khan," where he describes the palace in Xanadu as ". . . a miracle of rare device/A sunny pleasure dome with caves of ice!" When I look back on the wonders of Mr. Wilkerson's classroom, that's what I imagine. It was my own personal Xanadu.—*Maya Ajmera*

A LAW UNTO HIMSELF

Law school at Fordham University was a difficult period in my life. I didn't always fit in with my self-assured, overachieving classmates, some of whom would have evicted their own mothers to make the partnership track at one of the so-called "white-shoe" firms.

Abe Abramovsky, professor of criminal law, was more gumshoe than white shoe. At six-foot-two and 250 pounds, Abe really was larger than life. His legendary contacts in law enforcement and the defense bar, along with his thriving private practice in criminal law, lent him a film noir image. Attired in a brownish-gray London Fog raincoat, Marlboro cigarette in hand—he chain-smoked obsessively—he could have stepped out of the pages of a Raymond Chandler novel or the frame of a Quentin Tarantino or Coen Brothers film.

A genuine man of the people, Abe taught me that the true function of law is the defense of individual rights and unpopular causes. Abe was a liberal in the classic sense, far removed from the tedious political correctness of most of today's pundits and academics. (Indeed, Abe's chain-smoking constantly ran afoul of the student-faculty thought police.) He taught me to look beyond society's cant, to consider the facts above all else. And to discard ideology and theory when they fail, as they frequently do, to explain the facts.

As his research assistant and later, working with him on cases, I met an array of colorful characters—writers, Nazi hunters, prosecutors, judges, defenders, FBI agents, NYPD cops, and even the occasional target of an investigation. Abe often invited prominent members of the prosecutorial, judicial, investigatory, and defense communities to guest lecture in his class. He encouraged me to teach and to write—two activities I love above all others—and helped me understand that hard work and perseverance can overcome any obstacle. In short, Abe gave me affirmation when I needed it most.—*Daniel McLane*

GOOD-BYE TO PANTYHOSE

In 1976 I was a Senior V.P. Associate Creative Director at a mega-ad agency making a ton of money but crying every morning when I pulled up my pantyhose. One Sunday, I had a bizarre experience with my son in the park. I kept telling the story to people. The more I told it, the more polished it got. I felt I had to write it.

At that time, the top fiction gurus in New York City were Sidney Offit at the New School for Social Research, J. R. Humphreys at Columbia's School of General Studies, and Gordon Lish at his dining-room table. So I took Sid's class and wrote my story. I got an agent. I was hooked. Sid had a hard and fast rule, though: nobody took his course twice. I loved Lish, but he was pricey. Since my husband was a professor at Columbia, I could take J. R. Humphreys' workshop for free.

And so I did. For the next eleven years.

There were only two rules:

Rule 1: Don't look at the author when critiquing the work.

Rule 2: Start with what you like about the piece because if you start with what you don't like, you might never get around to what you like.

That was it. Two.

Gerard Shyne, who wrote the novel *Under the Influence of Mae*, used to say, "I just write to make Mr. Humphreys laugh." Dick had magic. I don't know how he did it, but he made you feel free to take risks, free to fail. He showed you what was good in your risks and failures and somehow you managed to write the damnedest stuff. Dick always knew what you were trying to do even if you didn't. I'd look at what I wrote and think, "What is this?" or "That came out of me?"

He critiqued students' work on paper he was recycling, so you'd get a snippet of his manuscript on the back of yours. Here's what Dick clipped to my story, "Mystery Salad," which was later singled out by *The New York Times* as the best story in my book, *All It Takes*. "Patty, the subject matter in this piece—and it's wonderful—is the visit to the old lady. Pull your frame in around the visit; otherwise, it's like a family photograph with too much foreground and background."

And this was printed on the other side of the paper: "He has never brought it up again. I see him once a week, and I suspect he's waiting for me to. I'll be damned if I'll bring it up. This may be called resistance, but to hell with it. I hate tricks and Newman is full of them—that grandfather's clock with the hands in his living room."

This is what that piece of paper did: It encouraged me, told me what my story was about and what to do with it. On the flip side, I got a gift, a compelling, well crafted paragraph from Dick's work in progress. My favorite samples had editing marks so I could see his mind at work.

Dick midwifed my first three books. When they were published, people began asking me to teach. I didn't see how I could do what he did. Then I looked through eleven years of notebooks and thought, Maybe I can pass this on. Maybe I can do for somebody else what Dick did for me. The same voice that whispers in my ear when I write talks to me when I teach. Here's what it says:

"It's not what can or can't be done. It's what you can get away with."

"Originality is just being yourself."

"If it's any good, you can't control it a hundred percent."

"Intellect is the censor. Emotion supplies the raw material."

"Let the book find its own way. When the first draft is finished, you'll find the beginning."

"The best way to write fiction is not to think about writing fiction."

"You don't have to understand a story when you write it. Emotion is a form of thought and that is its meaning."

"Explanations don't move us. Imagery does."

When *The New York Times Magazine* called and asked me to do an "On Language" column while William Safire was on vacation, I was paralyzed. I hurled myself into the tar pit of research. The more research I did, the worse it got. Then I remembered "Originality is just being yourself." I tore up the research and started writing. *The Times* didn't want me to write like William Safire. They wanted me to write like me. Dick gave me the courage to do that.

When he left Columbia, I left my job. I haven't worn pantyhose since 1988.—*Patricia Volk*

THE MUSIC MAN

I spent my eighth- and ninth-grade school years from September 1946 through June 1948 in the Jackson Township School District in Grove City, Ohio. I had come from Cleveland, with its modern, sophisticated educational program, and I looked despairingly upon this small, farm-serving school in a town of 2,500 people. But in this unlikely place, I found a teacher who would leave an indelible impression upon me, provide me with a fundamental knowledge of music notation, build my confidence as a musician, and, most important, imbue me with a love of and appreciation for fine music. This remarkable man, not yet thirty years old, was Richard L. Harris.

Under his tutelage, the eighth-grade class began learning nineteenth-century American music, most notably that of Stephen Foster. Everyone participated. It was impossible to resist the excitement that Mr. Harris generated.

I was a loud and vociferous singer, full of self-confidence and eager to show this man how much I enjoyed his classes. He soon had me singing solos (in my still unchanged alto range), but he had even bigger plans for me. There was a huge hole in his orchestra and band: there were no French horn players. I took to the instrument immediately, and for the next several weeks, Mr. Harris devoted after-school and even weekend hours to my musical education. He did not simply teach me how to play the horn, he taught me the rudiments of the musical language, scales, meters, rhythms, and how to produce the sounds both with the horn and with my voice. Within a very short time, I was in both the band and the orchestra, and in ninth grade (by which time my voice had dropped to tenor), the chorus as well.

But even chorus was not enough. Mr. Harris organized a male quartet with me as first tenor. Later in the year when my voice dropped some more, he expanded the group into a double quartet, and I switched to second tenor. Meanwhile, I was still studying the French horn and preparing a solo for the district music competitions.

Astonishingly, I was not the only one who received this kind of attention from Mr. Harris, nor did he cater only to those with obvious musical aptitude. My friend Jim could not sing on pitch at first, but he loved music. Mr. Harris put a sousaphone around Jim's head and showed him how to blow the basic open tones that everyone associated with the old Lifebuoy soap commercial: "BO." From that simple beginning, thanks to Mr. Harris's devotion, Jim became an accomplished tuba player and singer. Another student, Merritt, had a wonderful singing voice and a terrible stutter. Since he did not stutter when he sang, Mr. Harris prevailed upon his fellow teachers to let Merritt sing whenever he needed to communicate in class. His speech problem improved dramatically.

When I look back on this musical experience, I marvel at Richard Harris's accomplishments at this tiny school. He had well over one hundred students involved in his band, orchestra, and chorus—more than a third of the total student body. When he finished with these students, many were on their way to becoming accomplished musicians. By the time I was in tenth grade, in another school, I had vowed I would become a music teacher.

My stint as a high school music teacher was a short one, but I retained the love and appreciation of fine music as a choral conductor, choral singer, and creative listener. Music has sustained me spiritually and emotionally over the half-century since ninth grade. By filling my ears with glorious sounds, Richard Harris opened the door to my soul.
—*Ronald C. Harm*

FOLLOWING THE LEADER

The only worthwhile skill I learned in high school was how to type. The school administrators thought I took the course because that's where the girls were. They were correct—but I did learn to type. Otherwise, I saved my wits for more important things than education. I played football. I worked. I belonged to a fraternity. I went out with girls. Occasionally, I had a beer. When I realized I could memorize a deck of cards, I started gambling.

I lived in northern New Jersey, but it was not uncommon for me to cut school and go to Yankee Stadium or Ebbets Field with a couple of friends. This was just before the development of suburbs, so we could travel everywhere by public transportation. We were free spirits: we saw a Yankees game where Mickey Mantle came out and replaced Joe DiMaggio. And we cut school for a game against the St. Louis Browns, when the Yankees came back from a road trip with maybe an eighteen-game winning streak. Then Satchel Paige ambled out of the bullpen, threw the fastest strikes I've ever seen, and retired the Yanks.

Clearly, school work was not high on my list of priorities. The guidance counselor thought college would be a waste of my parents' money. I had no idea what I wanted to do, but my father was a pharmacist, and my older brother had just graduated from The Philadelphia College of Pharmacy and Science. So I applied, and as a sibling was automatically accepted—once I sent in a hundred dollar deposit.

I entered pharmacy school in 1954. By then, I'd met Sima, who would become my wife (she was sixteen, I was seventeen). Her father, three uncles, and an aunt were all pharmacists, and I wanted to impress her. So for the first time in my life, I became a serious student. I stopped drinking and gambling, and I wore a tie to class.

But, in truth, pharmacy school was not very challenging, and I began to wonder what I was doing there. I still didn't have the foggiest idea what I wanted to do with my life. Then, in my junior year, I started a two-year course in pharmacology, which is the basis of therapeutics and the mechanisms of drug action, and the most intellectually challenging of any subject in pharmacy school. To my immense good fortune, the course was taught by a splendid teacher named G. Victor Rossi.

To this day, Rossi remains the best public speaker I have ever encountered: his lectures were thoughtfully organized and well-written, they complemented the textbook, and they were laced with humor—not the jocular sort but the kind that arises naturally in the context of a topic.

He would hold the class spellbound with his elegant speech and fluid way of working on the blackboard. It was almost hypnotic, and very entertaining. He set an incredibly high standard—I'd say he directed the course to the top third of the class—and you had to be very, very quick at taking notes. It soon became apparent that reading the textbook was not enough; students had to be on top of the lectures. In most classes, I preferred to sit in the back; in Rossi's class, I fought for a front-row seat.

Rossi got sick one semester and we missed some lectures. It was just before an exam, so the test on that material was canceled. I was actually disappointed—the subject was estrogen and androgen pharmacology and therapeutics—so I went and read about it on my own. That's when I realized that, without his remarkable lectures to steer me, I had a much tougher time learning the subject.

Pharmacology may seem like a dry topic, but it isn't. Even in medical school, it is understood that drugs are the tools with which you attack disease. So dissecting drug mechanisms is fascinating work. I decided to pursue pharmacology in graduate school, but the only place I applied was The Philadelphia College of Pharmacy and Science—just so I could continue to study with Rossi. If I didn't get accepted, I wasn't going to go anywhere at all. I did get in, however, and I began to probe even more deeply. .

I also worked in Rossi's laboratory, which housed a magnificent file of reprints (he was always well-read and up-to-date on the literature). Perusing his files one day, I became intrigued by a paper on how new-born animals lack the liver enzyme that metabolizes drugs, by a fellow named Axelrod, who went on to win the Nobel Prize in 1970. There were also papers by Bernard B. Brodie, who did much of the pioneering work on drug metabolism. Looking at those reprints I recognized, finally, that this was the area in which I wanted to specialize. Rossi agreed.

After I got a master's degree with Rossi, I went to the University of Maryland Medical School to finish my Ph.D. Years of teaching followed, including twenty-five years at Washington University Medical School in St. Louis, where I headed the pharmacology department.

From the beginning, my teaching style mimicked Rossi's—I was very conscious of making eye contact, moving swiftly across blackboards, and using well-placed humor—and some of his aptitude must have rubbed off, because over the years at Washington U., I won the Teacher of the Year prize five times.

The focus of Rossi's career was lecturing and teaching. My own eventually took a different direction. Now I'm a member of the National Academy of Science, Chief Scientist of Monsanto, and the President and Head of Research and Development at our pharmaceutical company,

Searle. I have 2,000 scientists who work with me. Celebrex, a new drug that safely treats arthritis, was born in my laboratory at Washington University and developed over the following ten years with some of my colleagues from Washington U. and more than one hundred people from Searle. It's a major advance in arthritis treatment, and in its first three months of FDA approval, there were over two million prescriptions written. It's one of the most successful launches ever.

And I owe it all to Rossi. If he had been a botanist, I'd now be chasing after plant genes to improve the quality and safety of foods. I would have followed him anywhere.—*Philip Needleman*

STEEL MAGNOLIA

When I first heard Lillie Margaret Lazaruk's voice, I thought of magnolia trees and Spanish moss. My second thought was that her accent had to be fake. But as soon as I met her, I knew better. There was not a single shred of phoniness about this new college administrator at my urban ghetto community college in the mid-1970s.

Maybe fifty, she was tall and thin with fine brown hair, cut short in a no-fuss do. Her sedate, tasteful clothes were from Talbot's, mostly in grays and tans. Nothing about her screamed. Ever. Harsh New England winters, so different from the southern climes she was accustomed to, led her to wear pullovers and cardigans or shamefully soft paisley shawls. She took sick easily: she had only to cough or complain of a scratchy throat and I'd be brewing herbal teas and home remedies. Awed by her power, I attached myself to her, first as a student worker and then later as one of her many protégés.

That silky southern voice, I soon discovered, artfully concealed a will of feminist steel. I watched her grow ever more invigorated as she butted heads with the stagnant white male bureaucrats in college administration. She did not hesitate to call attention to their cronyism, their closed, old-boy network of power lunches and workouts at the health club. Armed only with charm and drive, she wrangled the necessary funds to establish a Women's Center at the college. With that coup, she was able to consolidate her power base, marshal her burgeoning band of feminist student followers, and lobby for an on-site child-care center, Women's History Month celebrations, and—scariest of all to the embattled men—equal pay for equal work.

Against whatever status quo the men were busy defending, she made thoughtful, rational arguments. She was wily, masterfully Machiavellian. She enlisted the disgruntled and disenfranchised in her ongoing battles, using what little free time she had to back the countless movements on campus aimed at improving women's lives. Somehow, she also managed to carve out time for her husband and son.

With her encouragement and guidance, I and many others she mentored pursued degrees in higher education administration. Slowly, in our own ways, we carried on the fight to make women's voices heard and heeded in colleges across America. In my first position, I often felt isolated and alone. But then I'd hear Lillie Margaret whispering her hard-won wisdom in my ear, like a guardian angel.

Relying on the secret arsenal of weapons I'd seen her wield, I managed to effect much-needed changes on my own campus. And during my two decades as a college administrator, I have always made time to mentor a female student. I only hope that I can offer her the same kind of powerful inspiration that Lillie Margaret offered me.—*Ruth Cash-Smith*

MY HIGH-SCHOOL LATIN TEACHER

The Romans were his heroes.
He kept Caesar's Gallic Wars

in his inside breast pocket
even after we'd finished Virgil
and gone on to Seneca's Moral Essays.
In class, I'd study the stripes
on his three-piece suit, his belt half hidden by his belly,
wondered what he was like when
he was in high school, whether a girl
had written his name over and over
on the cover of her biology book.
Perhaps his father had cuffed him
and called him hopeless.
I don't remember his name.
But I do remember feeling sad
for his small eyes, his uncertain
mouth. I wanted to know everything
he knew. At lunch he'd sit alone under
the please be courteous and neat *sign*
at the back of the cafeteria,
holding his dog-eared copy of Caesar
as if it were someone's hand.

—Pam Bernard

63

KIND HEARTS AND CORNETS

Except during the two years' time I spent in parochial school in Boston, Lemuel Doakes, the band director, was my first black male teacher. Because of his outstanding talents as a musician and teacher, he knew how to inspire the rest of us. Without actually using words, he had the ability to make us think, "Hey, I can do it. If I can, so can you." If I ever met a person who lived by the principle of giving one's best, it was Lemuel Doakes.

The kindest thing that I can say about our band at the time Mr. Doakes came to Southwestern High School is that it was not very good, especially the marching band. That did not distress Mr. Doakes. "I don't care what you were and I don't care what you weren't," he said. "What you are going to be is the best marching band in the city of Detroit. The best in the state of Michigan! Maybe the best in the United States!"

I cannot speak for the others, but I can tell you that he made me believe we could be the best—no, that we would be the best once he taught us. In the space of one school year, Lemuel Doakes took a ragtag marching band and made us into a first-class choreographic troupe.

Soon Mr. Doakes had us effectively competing with the best bands in the city. When I was in eleventh grade, we were selected to march in the Memorial Day Parade—quite an honor for us. Since then I have had several proud moments in my life, but none that made me feel happier or more self-assured than that parade day. Lemuel Doakes is the one who made us good, because he would not let us settle for just being all right or average.

Lemuel Doakes did one other thing in my life, something for which I will always be thankful. In elementary school, I had started to learn to play the clarinet. Then I switched to the cornet. When Mr. Doakes came, he said, "Ben, why don't you learn to play the baritone? I think you'd do well at it."

Of course, I switched. He was right; I took to the baritone easily. I don't know why he had me learn other instruments, but I do know that every time he suggested anything, I took it as a command. Each time I did well, my confidence grew just one more degree toward attaining a strong sense of self-achievement.

Mr. Doakes recognized that I had substantial musical talent and he frequently encouraged me. Yet, despite all the encouragement and the demand for perfection, he would not allow me or any of the others to put so much time into our practice that we let down on our academic work.

Just before we were to march in the Memorial Day Parade, I found myself in a real bind. I had taken on a science project that was demanding a large block of my time, and I was not sure whether I should stay with the project or spend the time practicing for the band competition. I do not recall whether I told Mr. Doakes or if he figured it out, but he called me aside to tell me, "Ben you've had enough practice today. You go work on your other subjects."

Impressive as that was, he did something else that impressed me even more. In Michigan, there is a special summer-long music program for gifted students. To get into the program, gifted students, before trying out, have to have the recommendation of their band teacher, a fairly high grade-point average, and be proficient with an instrument. If selected, they go to the prestigious Interlochen Music Camp for the summer. After heavy-duty instruction, these gifted musicians travel across the country and play under famous directors.

That it reflects favorably upon any band teacher whose students are accepted into this program goes without saying. When I was in the eleventh grade, Mr. Doakes spoke to the entire band about the Interlochen scholarships, how important they are, and the invaluable training that students receive. After explaining the rules for eligibility, he said, "And here at Southwestern High School four of you are eligible.

And they are . . . ." He made a big thing out of calling out our names, one at a time, and encouraging applause after each name.

Feeling really proud that Mr. Doakes thought I was good enough to be one of the eligible four, I was eager to try out. After the band session I asked him for more information about the scholarship. Everything he said made me more excited about competing. "And you think I'm good enough? That I could win?"

"Yes, Ben," said, "I think you're good enough. No question in my mind about that."

"Then you'll recommend me?"

Slowly he shook his head before he said, "I can't. It wouldn't be right."

"But you just said—"

"Ben, you're doing well in your academic work. I happen to know that you're right at the top of your class in every subject. You've told me that you want to be a doctor. That is what you want, isn't it?"

"Absolutely—"

"Then this scholarship isn't right for you," he said. "You have to choose one or the other."

I stared at him, hardly able to believe those words. "Look, Mr. Doakes, let me try. Maybe I could do both things—you know, work hard on my academic subjects and work hard with my music."

Very wisely he said, "No, Ben. Interlochen has an extremely demanding program. It would drain you of all your time and energy. You'll have to make a decision to do one or the other. I think your career is obviously in the scientific or medical field and that you really should go for that instead of concentrating on a music scholarship."

"Thanks, Mr. Doakes. I'm sure you're right," I said, wiping the disappointment from my face. I had wanted the scholarship. Yet, as I walked away from him, I had to admit that he was right. Somewhere along the line I would have to make a choice anyway. He helped me make it. Seconds later, the sense of disappointment gave way to genuine happiness. He cares about me. He's interested in me and in what happens to me. Being fairly naive and only sixteen years old, I don't think I realized how unselfishly he had acted. Except for my mother, nobody I knew had been more interested in me than in their own advancement. His unselfishness made me respect him as a great-hearted man.—*Ben Carson, M.D.*

COMPLEX ROOTS AND OTHER MYSTERIES

I had always been a good math student in high school, and in my last semester I signed up for advanced algebra, hoping to be challenged by some hard stuff. But my favorite math teacher, Mr. Cohen, barely got started in the semester when he fell ill and the class was taken over by a substitute—the gym teacher. She was a perfectly nice person, but she knew nothing about algebra, advanced or otherwise. She would come in to class every day in her gym outfit and call for volunteers to go to the blackboard and write out the answers to the homework assignment. Then she'd ask the rest of us if we disagreed with what was on the board. It was pretty clear that she was just stalling for time until Mr. Cohen returned. So were we all.

But he didn't come back, and pretty soon I was the only one volunteering. This was fine with the teacher, and it simplified things for the rest of us. In effect, I was teaching the class. One day the vice-principal summoned me to his office. I went with trepidation, but all he wanted to tell me was that Mr. Cohen's wife had called to say that he was very sick and to ask if I would like to visit him in their apartment.

That afternoon, I took a series of buses to Mr. Cohen's home in Flushing. My family had moved from this Queens neighborhood—with its overcrowded working-class apartment houses, its loud overhead subway trains coming and going all day and night, its street-floor stores and its slums—around the time I was born, relocating to the comparatively luxurious area of Douglaston Manor.

When I finally buzzed the doorbell of the old apartment house atop a row of shabby stores, Mrs. Cohen pulled me aside to warn me about her husband's condition. "He can't talk yet. The doctors say he'll get his voice back, but right now . . . ." She brightened. "It will just make his day that you're here. He's mentioned you as one of his best students."

I barely recognized him. Propped in a large overstuffed chair with a blanket covering his lap, he looked old, shriveled up, diminished. His shaking hands tried to smooth the pages of *The New York Times*.

We sat there. He stared at me. I had no idea what to do. Finally, he picked up a pad and wrote a message, slowly and unsteadily: "Tell me about the algebra class." So I did, explaining how I came to be teaching the class. I would say a few things, and then he would slowly write a question on his pad, tear off the note and hand it to me. I would respond. Slowly we managed to communicate.

After a while his wife reappeared. "We don't want to tire Charles out on his first day, Aaron." She winked at me. "Come into the kitchen." She pulled a plate of cakes out of her oven. I ate one, and then another. Boy, were they delicious! She scurried happily around her tiny kitchen—much smaller than the one we had at home, the one Mom was always complaining about. Wait till I tell her about this one, I thought.

Then I realized I wasn't going to tell Mom or anybody about these people's kitchen, or even this visit. I figured I'd just say I had to stay after school for something. As it turned out, nobody asked.

I returned to the Cohens' apartment later that week. Mr. Cohen had our advanced algebra text on his lapboard. "What page are you up to?" he wrote. I showed him. Another note: "State the root theorem." I did: Whenever x=r solves the polynomial, then (x - r) divides the polynomial. "Prove it," he scribbled. I did. I stared at the book; the author was Aaron Cohen. He'd written our textbook! Why had I never noticed?

And so we continued. He would ask me about equations; when I was puzzled, he'd give me a hint. And always, Mrs. Cohen would eventually interrupt to take me into the kitchen for some of her exquisite cakes. She never sent me off without a bundle of them for the trip back.

My visits became a regular pattern. As sick as he was, and unable to talk, you would have thought that Mr. Cohen would be unable to explain anything to anybody. But he would scribble his short questions and show me the key ideas in his book, step by step. In this way, he taught me about imaginary numbers, how to graph complex numbers, and what happens to these complex numbers when you multiply them together.

One day, he wasn't there. "He's back at Flushing Hospital, for tests,"

Mrs. Cohen said. "He's getting better, though, day by day. Can't you tell?" Not knowing what to say, I nodded. I could see she was anxious. She went back to her baking in the kitchen, while I looked around their small living room, cluttered with books from floor to ceiling. All kinds of books, mostly in German (I could tell by the old-fashioned script). But one shelf was in a strange language—I guessed it was Hebrew. Lots of Bibles, in different languages. Philosophy books. Art books. A whole section on astronomy. And, of course, math books, really advanced ones on topics I had never heard of before. It had never occurred to me that a high-school teacher could be so smart.

I noticed, in some, inscriptions that noted where and when he had bought the book. "Heidelberg, August 1935." Wasn't that during the time of Hitler? Wouldn't that have been a hard time for a Jewish math teacher? Another book: "Berlin, October 1937." God, did he stay in Germany? "Leipzig, January 1938." How did he ever get out of Hitler's clutches? I searched the books for more inscriptions, trying to piece together the details of his life. January 1939 was the last date. He must have left soon after that. I couldn't see any signs that the Cohens had children. Might they have—only the children didn't make it to America?

To my surprise, Mr. Cohen did get better. He could get up from his chair, and he even began to talk, quietly at first, then with more energy.

One day, as we were discussing complex roots of polynomials, he began to look through his bookshelf; he took down a very slim leather-bound book and handed it to me. "Here. Galois's theory of equations. Amazing for a young man to write on his twenty-first birthday. I feel I owe you something precious. You can learn this on your own."

I assured him he didn't owe me anything, but he insisted. I couldn't understand much, because it was in French, but in the weeks ahead, I managed to plow through it, with the help of a French-English dictionary that Mr. Cohen gave me. It turned out that mathematical French is simple. The Galois theorems, on the other hand, are not.

I ended up teaching the entire semester's course. We even covered more of the syllabus than was required. I say "we" because it really was a joint effort, in spite of the fact that Mr. Cohen never actually appeared in the classroom.

After five years of studying engineering physics and later, theoretical physics, I entered Cornell graduate school to study abstract mathematics. I finally learned Galois theory, and a lot more field theory besides. And I worked on my thesis in Lie algebras, which drew on materials that were solely in French. It is possible, of course, that I would have done all this had I never met Aaron Cohen. But I don't think so.—*Charles Haynie*

CHAPTER THREE

Throw Out the Rule Books

An early scene in the movie *Mr. Holland's Opus* shows Richard Dreyfuss standing before a roomful of blank-faced, bored students. "Who can tell me what music is?" he asks eagerly. His questions are met with polite silence. The students are not stupid; they are not disruptive, rude, or clownish. But they are a teacher's worst nightmare, far more frightening than a young rebel bent on confrontation, for their apathy is the measure of his failure.

Proficiency in one's subject is (or should be) a given, but that's not what makes a great teacher. If teachers cannot engage their students, they may as well talk to the wall. And to engage their students, they sometimes have to forget the format, throw out the syllabus, vacate the classroom. That is why, in the stories in this chapter, the teachers take their students on day trips to New York City, accept reports written in rhyming couplets, or simply read aloud to their classes, letting the gorgeous words sink deep into the minds of their listeners.

Such teachers may not always have perfect order in their classrooms, but that's not what matters to them. They know that true learning seldom follows all the rules.

HIS VOICE WAS FULL OF MEANING . . .

There is a whole generation of Miamians who can quote from memory Thomas Mann's paragraph on the human eye from *The Confessions of Felix Krull*. This is because twenty-five years ago, a Miami Springs High School teacher named Martin Obrentz lovingly read the entire novella aloud to the normally unruly mix of teenagers who made up his English classes. He devoted an entire class period to that memorable passage alone. In the process, he instilled in all of us—those who were college-bound as well as the equal number headed for blue-collar jobs—a love of language and literature that has lasted a lifetime.

I remember my first day in his class. Mr. Obrentz fit the mold of the absent-minded professor—disheveled hair, thick glasses—but it was his rich, deeply sonorous voice that commanded our attention. There was little talk of grammar, multiple-choice tests, SAT preparation. We would be expected to read a lot inside and outside of class and write essays on everything. This year, tenth grade, was world literature, so each nine-week period would be devoted to a theme—the Russian novel, the *Bildungsroman*, Existentialism. Based on what he thought we needed, Mr. Obrentz would assign different books to each of us.

The personalized assignments turned out to be a treat. When other teachers in the department were rhapsodizing about *Jonathan Livingston Seagull*, Mr. Obrentz was assigning *Oblomov*. Another assignment entailed reading multiple works by Bertolt Brecht. Once we were all assigned Holocaust-related reading—I got the book *Treblinka*—and I realized that through literature, we got a heady dose of history too. We devoted a whole nine weeks to *Anna Karenina*. As a result, many of us soon turned to *War and Peace*, because now we were hooked on books that, as Mr. Obrentz put it, "you want to open every day and say, 'How's the family?'" He was always genuinely interested in our reactions to particular authors or books, often smiling knowingly because he had made the right choice. Somehow, for example, he knew that I would be smitten with Scott Fitzgerald.

Mr. Obrentz's storytelling skills were carefully honed. All of us remember his colorful anecdotes, his occasionally risqué stories (we felt so grown up being included in them!), his culturally rich references that revealed his astonishing depth of knowledge of history, politics and languages—French, German ("just Yiddish ironed out"), some Russian, and even some Spanish. In a school with only a handful of Jewish students, he happily shared his own Judaism, even introducing us to the Middle Eastern sweet called halvah for our National Honor Society fundraisers, of which he was the faculty sponsor. Halvah quickly beat out doughnuts and Hershey's Almond bars as our top-selling snack.

But the most remarkable thing about Mr. Obrentz was the way he taught literature. He simply read the entire book aloud in class. To spend nine weeks on *The Great Gatsby*—what an unthinkable luxury! Yet daily we listened, intent, dreamy, relishing the way he lingered on lines like "Her voice was full of money" or catching the humor as he recited the names of Jay Gatsby's party guests. Hearing the novel read aloud opened our youthful minds to every nuance and cemented the story in our consciousness.

After twenty-five years, I am still in touch with Mr. Obrentz. So are many other former students. We have marathon conversations that cover books, movies, travels, discoveries. I had to call him immediately after reading Vladimir Nabokov's great masterwork, *Lolita*, to chide him for not having ever assigned it to me. He chuckled—a teenager would not have gotten out of it what a forty-year-old could. Of course he was right.

I can only hope my teenage daughter will have a teacher like Martin Obrentz one day. So far, it hasn't happened, and time grows short. Because of him, I read aloud to her often when she was small; sometimes I still do. Not long ago, I read her *The Great Gatsby*, and found myself, after all this time, hearing and imitating Martin Obrentz's resonant voice, making even clearer and more beautiful all those lovely, lovely words.—*Gretchen Schmidt*

THE DOODLE DEAL

I felt foolish just being there: a college senior with a bunch of sophomores, an art major in a two-credit educational sociology class of no real consequence, chosen mainly because the day and hour fit my schedule. Then again, I was feeling pretty foolish being in college at all. Not only had I never made a personal connection with any of my instructors, but I was even embroiled in battles with several in my search for something of personal relevance and an intellectual space in which to express myself. The education college of my university was notorious for its rather stodgy, boring courses—especially compared to the art college and its more liberal professors—and I settled patiently into my first-row seat for a tedious semester.

I can't say I noticed much of that first session, because I was engrossed in my usual practice of doodling. Near the end of the hour, the instructor, Dr. William Cave, asked to see me after class. I hadn't done anything. What did he want?

After the other students had cleared out, I stood uneasily at his desk. He smiled and complimented me on my doodles. Embarrassed, I offered that they ought to be decent; I was, after all, an art major.

"I'll make you a deal," Dr. Cave continued. "If you'll stop doodling in class, you can do anything you want as your curriculum."

I stared at him. "Anything?" I asked, incredulous.

"You can study whatever you want, write what you wish about it, turn in your papers however you like, and you don't have to take my exams. If you do whatever you do well, I'll give you a good grade."

I didn't hesitate, afraid he might come to his senses and withdraw this offer of a lifetime.

By that stage of my education, my expressive instincts had been pretty much stalemated by conflicts with my supposedly enlightened college professors. But if I could write here about whatever I wished, I sensed an opportunity. Since the class was about education, I started reflecting on my negative feelings about my experience in secondary school, eventually writing a piece proclaiming that the most noble students in my high school were the juvenile delinquents. That led to ruminations on an unhappy home life, and I began writing about all the difficulties I had experienced in my growing years. I ended up pouring more work into that little two-credit course than into my major studio classes or any other course I'd taken. I did in fact get a good grade, and I earned it. Dr. Cave even got one of my essays published.

When the semester ended, I could not stop writing, and it has continued to be my artistic outlet, beyond the graphics for which I was trained. Furthermore, the introspection begun in that class has burgeoned into a habitual practice that has healed me immeasurably. I wonder, on reflection, whether all this would have come to be had Dr. Cave not made me the doodle deal. —*Gordon Yaswen*

LUIGI'S SECOND ACT

Fresh from graduate school, Luigi Jannuzzi was assigned to teach the eleventh-grade World Religions class at the Catholic high school I attended in New Jersey. One look at this olive-skinned, small-framed man, with dark hair and very big, dark-brown eyes was all it took for me to develop an instant crush on him. In truth, Mr. Jannuzzi was a bit nerdy, but being a typical adolescent, I was smitten by his sensitive demeanor . . . and those big, brown, puppy-dog eyes.

But I was also captivated by his unorthodox and highly creative teaching style. Assigned the sweeping topic of World Religions, he made full use of his background as a playwright who had studied theology at Notre Dame. In an effort to "relate" to his students, this consummate intellectual tossed out some corny catch-phrases (a favorite was "Ohhh, yo-yo!"), but he was a brilliant lecturer. I'd always assumed that these dazzling (and hilarious) monologues were totally improvised until one day I snuck a peek into his marble composition book. I discovered that every last line had been written down—even the offhand remarks and seemingly spontaneous witticisms. But this information didn't de-romanticize him for me—he was too high on the pedestal to tumble down that easily. Rather, I felt in on his secret (even as I couldn't resist spilling it to other students).

Mr. Jannuzzi's reading assignments never failed to spark lively classroom debates. One book, especially, wowed us: Hermann Hesse's *Siddhartha*. At the time, it would never have occurred to me to think that a German writer's book about a Buddhist spiritual quest might be inauthentic. To me, it was stunningly original and a thrilling departure from my literature class, where a nun nicknamed "Sarge" presided over a tedious reading of *Beowulf*. *Siddhartha* touched my teenage soul, stirring my nascent desire to travel and learn about other cultures.

Mr. Jannuzzi represented everything that had been lacking in my first two years of high school. Now I was finally getting back to the creativity that had lain dormant for too long. But *Siddhartha* was just the beginning. Mr. Jannuzzi's other great enthusiasm was theater. Once, in acting class, he gave a side-splittingly funny demonstration of how to be, feel, and move like a piece of Jell-O. We then all tried to emulate his movements, wiggling around frantically until we broke out in uncontrollable laughter—especially when we tried to be Jell-O in motion, bobbing and jiggling across the room.

Our education extended well beyond our classroom walls. On several occasions, Mr. Jannuzzi took a handful of us on day trips into New York City, an hour away. Once we went to a Hare Krishna temple for the Sunday evening meal they offered. That was definitely a lesson in what religious group not to join—but, hey, the food was free.

On most of these trips, however, our main goal was "second-acting." To accomplish this, we would hang around Broadway theaters and pretend to be having a cigarette break at intermission with other theatergoers. (Mr. Jannuzzi didn't smoke, but he refrained from lecturing the few of us who did.) Then, when intermission ended, we'd sneak into the theater with the crowd and take any vacant seats (the ushers never bothered to check for tickets after intermission). In just this way, I saw half of several major Broadway shows. One especially lovely memory is when we met the late stage and screen actor Raul Julia backstage after *Dracula*. Julia proceeded to show us how the dry ice worked to create smoke. I'll never forget my fascination with this special-effects secret and the "real" actor who generously shared it with us.

By the end of our senior year, we were on first-name terms with "Luigi." Best of all, we had all turned eighteen, the drinking age in New Jersey at that time. This meant we could legally hang out and have the occasional beer with Luigi—an opportunity that allowed us the illusion that we were actually equals. In retrospect, I am incredibly impressed that Luigi (who, after all, wasn't much older than we were) never exploited his position of authority. Our trust in him was therefore true and lasting.

More important, that year he took a few of us into his theater fold. I acted in one of his plays that was staged at Rutgers University. Called *A Box Full of Hope*, it was a compilation of humorous, philosophical satires about the current state of the world. In one sketch, dressed in a black monk's robe, I played one of five "death brothers" who literally spelled out DEATH (I was the letter D). Excitedly, I waved my letter in the air while Death knocked at life's door.

For a high school student, appearing in a play that Luigi had written and directed himself was on an entirely different plane from the community theater I'd been acting in with my mom. The experience inspired me to believe that I, too, could do it all someday.

Luigi has been a teacher now for over seventeen years, the majority of which have been at my old high school. He's also had five plays published. I ended up teaching kids art and video, designing public programs for museums, and traveling in over three dozen countries in the decade after I graduated from college.

Not long ago, Luigi's and my paths crossed again. As a member of the board of directors for a New York City storytelling organization, I asked him to participate in an evening of "Teachers' Stories." Luigi told a hysterically funny and poignant story about taking kids on class trips, which he now does quite officially—complete with buses, permission slips, and bona-fide theater tickets! The crowd adored him.

After the program ended, I mustered the courage to confess my long-ago crush. Hearing this, Luigi turned red with embarrassment. (Could he never have suspected?) "Ohhh, oh-oh," he said. It was exactly the same intonation he used those many years ago when he'd utter his endearing

"Ohhh, yo-yo" to a group of eager, entranced teenagers.—*Pegi Vail*

THE STRAWBERRY AND MS. SWEERS

As a senior at New Trier Township High School in Winnetka, Illinois, I took a philosophy class that changed my life, woke me up, taught me more than anything else before or since. I can trace the defining moment to the day Ms. Sweers came to class with a flat of strawberries.

As she solemnly placed a strawberry on each of our desks, she warned us not to eat the fruit right away. We were instructed to take a full five minutes to experience the strawberry, without putting it in our mouths. She told us to look at it closely, smell it deeply, rub it against our cheeks, open ourselves to its berryness.

It was as if I had never seen a berry before in my life. All of a sudden, an intricate world of seed and leaf crease and red richer than any I had ever seen was revealed to me. When the five minutes were up, we were told to take another entire five minutes to eat the berry. We were to eat mindfully, in order to experience each flavor, each texture, as fully as possible. I felt my mouth wake up. Sweet and sour exploded on my tongue. I felt more alive than I'd ever felt. In ten minutes, I learned more than I had in all my other classes combined.

When we were finished eating our strawberries, the floppy crowns of leaves splayed on our desks, Ms. Sweers asked us to write a haiku about the experience, distilling our impressions into seventeen syllables. I don't recall my entire haiku, but one line was "A small heart beats in my mouth." A few kids said, "Ewwww," when I read that out loud, but it perfectly expressed how that strawberry came to life for me.

I love this exercise still. I once put together a performance piece in which I passed out strawberries and read Gary Snyder's poem, "Song of the Taste," while the audience explored the berries. I danced while they slowly ate, the smell of the berries rising around me.

I am so grateful for the strawberry Ms. Sweers placed on my desk those twelve years ago. With this gift, she issued my true wake-up call, sweetly guiding me to the heart of my own life.—*Gayle Brandeis*

CONFIDENCE IN COUPLETS

Mrs. Pardenek, my fifth-grade teacher at School #9 on Brighton Road in Clifton, New Jersey, was exceptional. She was pretty. Tall. Blond. Probably in her thirties, though at the time she seemed much older to me. She wore her hair in a flip, like Marlo Thomas in *That Girl*. You have to understand that Clifton in the 1960s was hardly an enlightened place. It was 99.9 percent white, with an unspoken but active policy to keep blacks out of housing and jobs. It was shockingly provincial, considering it was no more than a twenty-minute ride from New York City.

Occasionally, my mother would take me out of school to see the opera or ballet in Manhattan—experiences almost unheard of in Clifton. Once, my father, a research scientist, offered to come into my classroom and let kids look at cells under his microscope. The school administrators vetoed the idea because it wasn't in the curriculum.

We had art class once a week, and we painted or cut out Christmas ornaments or snowflakes and hung them in the window. Music class, which took place once a week in the second grade, consisted of a rotund schoolmarm playing the accordion while we sang. The only other arts I can remember were the *National Geographic* specials they showed in the auditorium whenever we couldn't go outside for recess. Now and then these nature films were replaced by cartoons.

I was a naturally creative person, but not only was creativity never nurtured in any way, it was actually discouraged. So when Mrs. Pardenek came along in the fifth grade, it was pure bliss. She liked and encouraged my artistic nature. When she discovered that I loved writing poetry, she did something that other Clifton teachers would never have thought of, let alone permitted. She let me write and deliver my history reports in rhyming couplets. I can still remember the opening of my report on evolution: "Early man looked just like an ape/ Boy, did he have a funny shape/ There were fourteen kinds of men, none the same/ And each of them had a different name."

She also gave me the lead in the fifth-grade class play. Today I make my living as a professional storyteller, and I'm convinced that this role started me on my road as a performer. My rival that year, Sue-Ann Marker, was the cutest girl in the class; all the boys loved her. In fact, they had come up with rankings: First Chick, Second Chick, Replacement Chick. Sue-Ann was always rated First Chick. I didn't even make the list. But when Mrs. Pardenek gave me the lead in *Living Up To Lincoln* and my mother rolled my hair in banana curls for the occasion, I briefly became one boy's Replacement Chick. It's true that the day after the performance, when my hair went back to normal, I was dropped from the list. But I'd won the lead in the play—all fifty-two lines' worth. It was quite a coup, and it did wonders for my confidence.

We all know, of course, that by the time a child enters the fifth grade, her personality is formed. But Mrs. Pardenek made me feel comfortable in mine. That kind of gift cannot be measured.—*Lisa Lipkin*

THE REAL THING

"I can't believe someone who would hang this incredible piece of work on the wall would put this piece of crap right next to it." The incredible piece of work that my fine-art photography professor was motioning toward was a photo I had taken of my parents in the backyard. There was a dark pole in the middle—one of the supporting beams of the patio on which I stood to take the picture—with my parents positioned on either side of it. "Look at the lines of despair in their faces. It's obvious that they're trapped in their lives." I looked at the five-by-seven black-and-white print with new eyes. My father was standing off to the side, staring into the distance with a slightly unfocused look. My mother was shielding her forehead with her hand. Her scrawny shoulders turned inward and her thin sweater was buttoned down the front.

With a dismissive wave of her hand, my teacher motioned to the photo hanging next to this. "And this piece of garbage, this kid smiling into the camera." The smiling kid was on her Big Wheel in an apartment parking lot, where I'd found her unattended and dangerously close to the highway. When I snapped the picture, the kid's mother was at home drinking her welfare check and smoking her way through a carton of Marlboros, all the while fretting that she had no money for groceries. This smiling kid had much more despair in her life than my parents did. But, of course, none of this could be seen in the Kodak moment pinned on the wall. It didn't matter: what thrilled me was being in the presence of a teacher so blithely confident of her own opinions.

The teacher's name was Nancy, and her students either hated her or loved her. I fell into the latter category. I loved the way her wiry mass of salt-and-pepper curls fell into her face when she talked and that she didn't care. I loved that she wore a sleeveless shirt under her overalls and that her bushy armpit hair stuck out when she gestured with her long skinny arms. And I especially loved that she used four-letter words emphatically, frequently, and with great aplomb.

It was rumored that she was rich—that she lived on an estate in Upper Bucks County previously owned by a world-famous ballet dancer. If I had found this to be true, I would only have loved her more for being so totally unaffected by her wealth. She was completely different from the other women teachers at my community college, who were so cautious in language, dress, and even, it seemed, their thoughts. In truth, I was more like them than I was like her. But I knew the real thing when

I saw it: I had a deep reverence for art, and she was no less than its personification.

As much as she made herself available to us—coaching us on darkroom techniques, critiquing our work, taking us to photography exhibitions in New York City—there was also something aloof and unapproachable about her. I admired her devotion to her art, the intense seriousness yet utter indifference to outcome with which she approached everything. But most of all I sensed her deep self-knowledge and awareness, and it was this that held the strongest pull for me. I wanted that, too, but at the time I didn't have a clue how to go after it.

One afternoon when I was hanging around after class, she gave me an odd look and asked if I wanted to come upstairs to her studio and see her new work. I knew such invitations were not offered lightly, and I was touched by her interest. But in the next moment, I balked. It was true that I was late to my work-study job, but more to the point, I was terrified of exploring the self I saw reflected in her. At nineteen, I clung to the hope and the fear that deep down I really wasn't like everyone else. The last thing I wanted to discover is that maybe I was.

As the years went by I slowly, one by one, unlocked those doors into who I was. But it was the art of seeing, which I learned from her, that sustained me through the journey.—*Janet Mason*

SIMPLE TO THE CORE

In twenty years of schooling, the most interesting class I ever had was a five-year course in the history of architecture that I took in the 1960s at the Pratt Institute in Brooklyn. The instructor was Sibyl Moholy-Nagy, an architectural critic and the widow of the great avant-garde Hungarian designer, painter, and photographer László Moholy-Nagy.

Professor Moholy-Nagy, who was one of Pratt's legendary teachers, was every bit as iconoclastic in her thinking as her husband, who was an early member of the Bauhaus school of architecture and one of the twentieth century's most influential figures in art education. One day in the third year of her course, Professor Moholy-Nagy announced to the class, "Students, you have three minutes to design a city." She looked at her wristwatch; exactly 180 seconds later, she said, "Pencils up—turn in your papers."

I have always remembered what I did in that tiny window of opportunity: I drew an apple with a crystal cube as its core. Several days later, Professor Moholy-Nagy asked me what I was thinking about when I did that. I responded that the crystal cube was capable of reflecting the universe and that cities need similar centers.

Her class and that lesson have continued to resonate throughout my life and in all the work I have done in experimental theater. Before it can be complex, theater must first be simple. This little three-minute exercise forced me to think in a big way, simply.—*Robert Wilson*

CHAPTER FOUR

The "Aha" Moment

Most of us can remember sitting catatonic at a school desk, lost in a thicket of misunderstanding and incomprehension—or perhaps merely bored. Then the teacher, with an offhand comment, suddenly makes Latin grammar—or algebra or philosophy or our own position in the scheme of things—click obediently into place. Perhaps we even see its beauty and symmetry. The moment, as Nora Ephron observes here in her story about her high school journalism teacher, can be "breathtaking . . . like those depictions in cartoons of a little electric bulb lighting up in the balloon above a character's head." After months, perhaps years, of not really getting it, we finally see what all the fuss is about.

Though almost all of us have had at least one such experience, in which understanding simply floods in, the teacher is often the last to know. For all those men and women who stand before a classroom of students wondering if anything they are saying is actually getting

94

through, the stories in this chapter serve as a vivid reminder of their profession's eternal power to transform.

GETTING TO THE POINT

Charles O. Simms, my journalism teacher at Beverly Hills High School, was the best teacher I ever had. On the first day of class, he set out to teach all of us how to write a lead—the first and most important paragraph of any news story. He wrote the words Who? What? When? Where? and Why? on the blackboard. Then, he proceeded to do what all journalism teachers do: He dictated a set of facts to us while we sat at our manual typewriters (this was back in the late fifties, you understand) and tried to pound out a lead.

The facts he dictated went something like this: "Kenneth L. Peters, the principal of Beverly Hills High School, announced today that the entire high school faculty will travel to Sacramento next Thursday for a colloquium in new teaching methods. Among the speakers will be anthropologist Margaret Mead, college president Dr. Robert Maynard Hutchins, and California Governor Edmund 'Pat' Brown."

The leads we wrote went something like this: "Governor Pat Brown,

Margaret Mead, and Robert Maynard Hutchins will address the Beverly Hills High School faculty Thursday in Sacramento . . . blah, blah, blah."

Basically, we all just took the facts, turned them ever so slightly around, and rewrote them. We rolled our sheets of paper out of the typewriters and passed them to the front of the classroom, where Mr. Simms quickly riffled through them. Then he looked up at us and announced, "The lead to the story is, 'There will be no school next Thursday.' "

It was a breathtaking moment. For me, it was exactly like those depictions in cartoons of a little electric bulb lighting up in the balloon above a character's head. In that instant, I realized that journalism was not just about regurgitating the facts but about figuring out the point. It wasn't enough to know the who, what, when, where, and why—you had to understand what it meant. And why it mattered.

For the rest of that school year, every single assignment Mr. Simms gave us had some secret, hidden point that we somehow had to figure out before we could write about it. It was a thrilling class, and largely because of it—and him—I became a journalist.—*Nora Ephron*

MR. PERFECT

When I flunked out of medical school back in 1952 (kind of on purpose), I was in bad shape. I'll never forget that last day, riding the El back down to the Loop to catch another train to the South Side to face my M.D. dad and my hysterical mother, who had invested themselves in my becoming a doctor as if their own lives were at stake.

My soul was steeped in the grayness of the Chicago sky. I felt spacy, crazy, a nobody, a canceled check. When I told my parents I'd torn up the final exam in biochemistry and I was going to study literature and be a writer, my perfectly manicured, permanent-waved mother uttered a single word—"Loser!"—and walked back into her bedroom and slammed the door.

I left home and got a job packing bibles on the South Side. That summer I reenrolled at Loyola University. My first class was in the English Romantic poets, taught by Professor Martin Svaglic—Mr. Perfect. Always the perfect overcoat, the perfect fedora, the perfect silk scarf.

The course itself was as tough as biochemistry. We immersed ourselves in Wordsworth, Keats, Shelley, and Byron. We read several of the big poems, like Byron's *Don Juan*, as well as the complete works of Keats. The final was a real killer. I did my best. All I could say was that I felt a lot more comfortable than I ever had in med school.

We had one last summing-up class the day after the final, and Svaglic brought in the results. As he handed back our tests, he said, "What I've done here was to use Hugh Fox's answers as the standard against which I graded everything else."

After being in the psychological gutter for months after my medical school debacle, it was as if the ground had split open. Suddenly, the sun was streaming in and the Angel of Life was lifting me, if not up to heaven, at least to ground level.

That last day, Svaglic left a white silk scarf behind on the desk. I picked it up after class, and that night, I called him at home.

"Professor Svaglic?"

"Martin? You mean Martin Svaglic?" asked a thickly accented voice on the other end.

"Yes," I answered. "Professor Martin Svaglic."

"He not here right now. At delicatessen. Be back soon. I father, his," the man said, and abruptly hung up.

I called back in half an hour and Professor Svaglic was home. I told him about the scarf and volunteered to bring it to his place.

"No, no, don't bother," he said in his almost Oxonian accent. "Just leave it in the Lost and Found in the library. I can pick it up there." A pause, and then, "Incidentally, thanks for caring. It's been fun to have you in class."

Click.

There were so many messages in this man, messages about past and present, about beginning again, moving on to new things. One message came through louder and clearer than all the rest: I was not my father.—*Hugh Fox*

SKY-BLUE PINK

"What would you call that color, Mom?" my daughter Nell asked, pointing at the late afternoon skyline filled with vibrant blues and pinks and softer hues of violet, rose and lavender.

"I've always called it sky-blue pink," I answered, remembering the man who had first used that phrase, as I always remember him when the sunset turns that special color.

It was the day of the eighth-grade graduation practice at Wynantskill School, the small public grade school in the little country town where I grew up. We were learning to march in cadence to "Pomp and Circumstance," played on a tinny old piano by the music teacher.

After we'd perfected our marching and our choral rendition of "You'll Never Walk Alone," it was time to talk about behavior and attire for graduation day. Our principal, Mr. Fred E. Gardner, took the microphone and asked for our silence and attention.

You could hear a pin drop in the auditorium when Mr. Gardner was in charge, for we both respected and feared him. His jowly, mustache-bedecked face was most often set in a glower, and at six-foot-four he towered above everyone else in the school, especially the students. If you were disrespectful to a teacher or mean to another kid, if you cheated on a test or "borrowed" someone else's lunch money, you could expect an invitation to Mr. Gardner's office.

But we liked him, too, for we knew he was on our side. Once, in third grade, I'd seen him break a desk in two with the slap of his hand as he emphatically fired a teacher who had been deliberately cruel to a child. Another time, when a boy appeared in school one morning covered with bruises from a harsh beating, it was Mr. Gardner who knocked on the parents' door, before the police or the welfare agency. The parents of that boy soon understood there would be no more beatings of any child who attended Fred Gardner's school.

"Tomorrow you will graduate from this school," he began. He looked around at the motley crew that comprised our eighth-grade class. We were all going in different directions: some to public high school in another town, some to a local military school, some to a parochial high school in the city, and some to a tech school. For a few kids, this graduation might be the only one. They would not get through high school, drawn to farm work like their fathers or dropping out to join the Army. Acknowledging our diversity, Mr. Gardner continued.

"I want you to have good memories of your years here and your graduation day, and I want you to look good. In accordance with tradition, the boys will wear white sports coats, the girls white dresses." This was not news to us, for we had all been preparing our ensembles for days. Still, someone had to ask the question. Sharon took the chance.

"Mr. Gardner, what if your dress has little pink buttons on it?"

"Sharon," our principal answered sternly, "is your dress white?"

She nodded.

"Well, then," Mr. Gardner replied, "I don't care if the buttons are sky-blue pink, as long as the dress is white."

One of the tough boys in the back of the auditorium raised his hand. "What is sky-blue pink, anyway? I never seen no color like that in my crayon box," he challenged, his voice taking an innocent tone to mask his wise-cracking question. A few girls dared to snicker.

Fred Gardner took off his glasses and massaged his brow. For a moment, we all thought he might tear off the stage and lift the wise-cracker right out of his seat and hurl him from the auditorium. Through the microphone we could all hear him take a deep breath.

"That's a good question, son," he said, surprising the troublemaker and ignoring the boy's bad grammar. "Let me see if I can explain. Some afternoon," he continued, "you will look at the sky just before sunset, and you will see a color you will never see in a Crayola box. You will see pinks and blues swirling together in such a way it almost doesn't look real. It will be a riot of color so beautiful it could take your breath away. I call that color sky-blue pink," he said.

"Any more questions?" No one dared to raise a hand. "All right, then. See you tomorrow. Four o'clock sharp." He turned and left the stage. As I watched him walk down the steps and leave the auditorium, I realized that this man we all feared and respected had a side that wasn't always apparent to the hooligans of our school—a gentle side that loved beauty. On the day before I graduated from eighth grade, I realized something about the complexities of human nature. In retrospect, I believe this was my first truly adult thought.—*Mickey Clement*

PERMISSION GRANTED

I don't remember the year, but I do remember everything else. I had recently quit dancing, a career I had been moving toward since the age of three. Apart from ballet, my life had revolved around my vain attempts to save my father, who had been in and out of drug rehab for as long as I could recall.

Nothing engaged me. Nothing moved me. Nothing mattered. I still lived in New York City, where I had grown up. I drifted in and out of classes at Hunter College. In and out of low-paying, temporary jobs. My life was static, and I didn't even really mind. Then for some reason—largely because it fit into my schedule—I stumbled into a college composition class. To my surprise, I kind of liked it.

About three weeks into the semester, my father relapsed . . . again. My entire focus shifted back to him. Back to his pitiful predicament and what I perceived to be yet another failure on my part. I stopped going to classes. Just stopped, without a word to anyone. This had happened before, and I was resigned to its being the shape of my life. Indeed, its familiarity was almost comforting. But this time, I told my composition teacher.

I figured that once she heard my tale of woe, she'd say I could drop the class without penalty. And that would have been enough.

But she didn't say what I'd anticipated. What she said was, "I can help you." I must have looked suspicious. Certainly, I felt that way.

She continued, "You can do one of two things: You can drop the class and go do what you have to do. Or I can help you put yourself in the center of your life." Myself at the center of my life? Instead of my father and his problems? The possibility had never occurred to me, nor had it ever been suggested by anyone else. The very idea was a revelation.

I think now that I chose to confide in Louise DeSalvo not because she had had similar experiences, or because it was part of her job as a teacher, but simply because I thought perhaps she could comprehend my situation without judgment. When she did, I finally reclaimed my life.

So how did she do it, you may be wondering. Was there some magic potion, some exercise, some special therapy? Of course not. It was simply hearing the words. It was, in effect, being given permission to live. I felt lifted, renewed, brought closer to the core of my being.

Maybe I didn't really need Louise DeSalvo. Maybe I would have found the courage on my own to finish school, move to California, and forge a new life for myself. Maybe. But I have no doubt that, without her, I would not possess the faith in humanity I have now, would not walk in the world the way I am able to now, would not be the woman I have become. Everything I am I owe to a teacher who, without even knowing me, made me see that I mattered.—*Marika Brussel*

FROM ROCKS TO RHYME

I'll never forget the day my college English professor read the poem that determined my fate. It was spring 1982. After a year of dabbling in a variety of subjects, I had finally settled on a geology major. Learning to distinguish between metamorphic and sedimentary rock formations, deciphering the meaning of layers in cuts along the road, were accomplishments of which I, a wife, mother, and returning student, was especially proud. Being a geologist had a certain ring to it. It meant adventure, prestige, and, quite possibly, a great deal of money.

In order to get my degree, of course, I had to take a number of classes outside my major. I had always done well in English, earning A's in high school and even tutoring other students who were struggling, so I welcomed the requirement—not because of great interest but because I thought the class would be easy.

That school day began like any other, with geology lab. We were studying topographic maps, which represent earthly structures with spiraling lines and concentric circles. From the beginning, I had been having trouble understanding the configurations and visualizing the earth below. The map was a flat surface while the earth was three-dimensional, and I could not mentally bridge that gap. Dizzy and starting to sweat, I looked around at the other students and saw no signs of confusion in their faces. They all appeared to be answering the assigned questions with ease. Meanwhile, I watched the clock, eagerly awaiting my escape. How, I wondered, could I ever be a geologist without grasping this most basic knowledge? I left the classroom bewildered.

Dragging myself to English, I contemplated dropping out of school. I had succumbed to the Peter Principle, I decided, rising to my level of incompetence. School was fun, but I was kidding myself if I believed it could ever be more. Why should I even bother going to class? But I was already at the door, and anyway, I needed to sit down.

Professor Heffernan, a wiry, middle-aged man with an edgy intensity, began class on time, as always. The topic of the day was the poetry of the nineteenth-century British poet Gerard Manley Hopkins. I was only half-listening as Professor Heffernan talked first about the poems' structure and then about the innovation for which Hopkins is known.

There he stood in his jeans and running shoes (he'd often mentioned his need for a daily run), completely unaware of my pain. A truly good teacher, I thought, would have picked up on it.

Despite my preoccupation, I perked up at bit as he recited the first lines of Hopkins's "Pied Beauty": "Glory be to God for dappled things/ For skies of couple-colour as a brinded cow;/ For rose-moles all in stipple upon trout that swim;/ Fresh-firecoal chestnut-falls; finches' wings . . ." I briefly marveled at the inventiveness of those words, the unique use of alliteration, the vivid imagery. By the time he had finished the poem, however, I was back to brooding.

But then came Hopkins's "Spring and Fall." "Margaret are you grieving/ Over Goldengrove unleaving?" began Professor Heffernan. The poem centers on Margaret, a young girl who sadly observes the falling of autumn leaves. The speaker initially wonders at her sorrow— "Leaves, like the things of man, you/ With your fresh thoughts care for, can you?"—but ultimately attributes it to an unconscious, "ghost guessed" recognition of her own inevitable death. The poem concludes with the line, "It is Margaret you mourn for."

Here Hopkins was at the height of his powers, and so was Professor Heffernan. Sitting on one of the desks, body contracted, voice resonant, he delivered the poem precisely as I imagined Hopkins would have decreed, illuminating with impassioned restraint the simultaneous loss and hope the poem expresses. Professor Heffernan, in fact, was the perfect vehicle for Hopkins's craft: his cadences, rhythm, and tone left me not dizzy or sweaty, but breathless.

Falling leaves. Now, these were symbols I could understand—symbols of life's brevity, of nature's tragedy as well as its beauty. With his reading of Hopkins, Professor Heffernan opened up a world, one in which I instantly knew I wanted to immerse myself. Immediately, I abandoned the lines on the map and embraced the lines on the page, lines whose meanings were not limited by terrestrial forms but liberated by the infinite range of human experience.

Today, nearly two decades later, I am a professor of literature myself. On my office wall hangs a hand-written version of "Spring and Fall," a gift from my husband and a daily reminder of the teacher who changed the course of my life. Some might say that anyone could have performed that reading, that I was ripe for a conversion. The latter is no doubt true, but I also know that only this particular man could have brought my conversion about. It was his interpretation that spoke so profoundly to me that day, taking me in a single, breathtaking moment from rocks to rhyme.—*Ona Russell*

ACTING THE PART

It was the end of the second semester of my freshman year in college, and I was taking the oral portion of our final Spanish exam. My teacher, Señor Lopez, began asking me a few questions in Spanish—testing my vocabulary, my command of the subjunctive, my comprehension of a paragraph he read aloud. And I answered back, also in Spanish.

I was nervous—I hated oral exams and could hardly wait for them to be over. But I was startled when after only two or three questions, Señor Lopez slapped his hand on the desk, looked me in the eye, and said, "I know you know this. You get A's on all your written exams. What I want to know is, how come you never talk in my class?"

"Uh . . . I don't know," I stammered. "I guess . . . I guess I'm just shy . . . I guess."

"Shy!?" he repeated, a little loudly. He stood up and started pacing. "Shy? What do you mean shy? What do you have to be shy about?"

I was silent.

He sat down again, in front of me. "You know what shyness is?" he asked, more gently now. "Shyness is a crutch!"

I don't remember much about the rest of the exam. I think Señor Lopez asked me another question or two, then let me go. Nothing he said to me that day was cruel or sadistic—just blunt. Yet I left his office deeply shaken. Señor Lopez had hit a nerve.

I had been plagued by shyness for as long as I could remember. I was afraid of opening my mouth around anyone but trusted friends, and was constantly intimidated by others. Because of my fears, I felt I had missed out on what people were always calling "the best years of my life." All through high school, I'd avoided dating and parties. Now, here I was in college, with a better-than-even chance that the rest of my years would be exactly the same.

But a crutch? That I didn't like. So I took Señor Lopez's words as a challenge. I vowed to change. But how?

I decided that I would act like someone who was not shy. If I could perform the part, I thought, like a role in a play, maybe somehow I could finally do all the things that I was so afraid of. It would be somebody else doing them—some character instead of me.

So I put on a mask and started behaving like a person who was extroverted and confident. And little by little, the mask began to merge with the inner me, until the line between them was a blur. I found myself routinely doing and saying things that once would have been alien.

I registered for an acting and directing class. To my horror, on the first day, the graduate-student instructor—like Señor Lopez, a young man who bubbled with energy—announced that much of the class would deal with improvisation. Nothing could have petrified me more: No written script to fall back on as a safety net! Every day I would walk into class trembling . . . and come out feeling great, just for having faced my fears. (I ended up earning an A.)

Even now, more than fifteen years later, I still struggle with my shy tendencies. Public speaking is still torture for me. But I am truly a different person from the diffident girl who took that oral Spanish exam. Yes, I still get afraid, but now I actually welcome the opportunity to plunge into scary waters and to rise above them.

Most of my newer friends these days find it hard to believe that I ever was that timid, terrified creature. That's when I tell them the story of my Spanish exam and of Señor Lopez, whose first name I don't remember and am not sure I ever knew. And of how he, without ever knowing it (I never saw or spoke to him again after that day) completely changed my life.—*Anne Newgarden*

READER, I MARRIED HER!

It was 1953, and Dwight D. Eisenhower was president. I was ten years old, the tallest kid in fourth grade, and in love. So was every other boy in my class—and not with one of the budding beauties we sat next to or square danced with in the gym, but with our teacher, Mrs. Greasehammer. What a name. Ah, yes, but what a teacher! Not only was she sweet, kind, and understanding, she was drop-dead beautiful.

Appropriately enough, Mrs. Greasehammer taught the second half of the fourth grade, which fell in the spring—a time when flowers were budding, the air was losing its winter chill, and the woolen wear of winter was being shed. And Mrs. Greasehammer was spring itself! A tall woman, with flowing red hair, she wore bright floral dresses, accented with color-coordinated jewelry, and high-heeled pumps that elevated her to the top of the blackboard. It was a delight to the senses just to look at her. However, this made it impossible to concentrate on, among other things, long division, the killer subject of fourth grade.

That year, I was chosen to be on the school safety patrol—an honor of sorts—and assigned to a corner next to the school. There I stood and guided children safely across the street. The best part of the assignment was not the status but the fact that I was on "the corner"—the same corner where Mrs. Greasehammer, in her bright red 1953 Packard convertible, would turn every morning on her way to the school parking lot. What a sight! As Mrs. Greasehammer honked and waved hello, I stood at attention, white belt across my chest, and waved back, all the while wishing I were in the seat next to her, bound for a wedding chapel.

The fourth grade ended and summer vacation arrived. My family moved and I started a new school in the fall. But my vision of the two of us together never completely faded.

Life went on, and in time some of my boyhood dreams were fulfilled and others were forgotten. It has been forty-four years since I last laid eyes on Mrs. Greasehammer, yet when I awoke today, for reasons I don't understand, a crystal-clear picture of her formed in my mind. That's when it hit me—my wife is beautiful, kind, and has a wonderful way with children. She dresses in a beguiling manner, drives a flashy blue convertible, and unbelievable as it may seem, teaches fourth grade. She captivates me and every other boy she meets. (Yes, I still think of myself as a boy.) In short, she is the reincarnation of Mrs. Greasehammer.

I always wanted to marry my fourth-grade teacher. Today, I realized that I did!—*Sander M. Fields*

CHAPTER FIVE

To Sir, With Love

Some teachers just seem to have a knack for empathy, for zeroing in our our inner longings, our ambitions, or the discontent that festers in our souls. By recognizing in us qualities the rest of the world has been more than happy to ignore, they validate our youthful existence and give us—to invoke an overused term—self-esteem. They do this not by cheap tricks or lavish but essentially empty praise, but by revealing to us what is best in ourselves and getting us to build on it. These are the teachers who make us a vital part of the class when nobody else thinks we are worth the effort, who shine a light on the darkness we carry inside us.

In such teachers we often find a kindred spirit, a long-sought soul-mate—and the affirmation can last a lifetime. For anyone who has ever felt misunderstood, out of place, or invisible, the exhilaration of finally finding someone who notices is heady indeed. These teachers glimpse the person we only *wish* we were, and we blossom in their gaze.

AT HOME ON THE COURT

I entered ninth grade with little hope that it would be better than seventh or eighth. My family had moved to Bellevue, Washington, two years earlier, midway through the 1961–62 school year. Up until that time, we had relocated every six months or so. My stepfather worked for the Washington Highway Department helping to build the interstates. As I-5 advanced south toward Seattle from Bellingham, my mother, three sisters, two brothers, and I had moved with him, like the migrant farm workers who followed the harvests in Washington State's berry fields and apple orchards.

My stepfather would come home exhausted and then leave for his second job, usually pumping gas at a local service station. My mother also worked, as much as a high-school dropout trying to raise six children could. (She'd had to quit school at thirteen to help support her family. By the time she was nineteen, she was divorced with two small kids—me and my older sister—and the only work she was able to find was as a maid, cleaning motel rooms.)

For a young boy with limited social skills, enrolling in two new schools every year was agony. I was always the new kid, always on the outside, always the brunt of jokes. The fact that I was a mediocre student didn't help. As I bounced from school to school, I learned that friends, for me anyway, were nearly impossible to make and keep. As a result, I developed a deep longing to find a place to fit in.

Bellevue was becoming the newest bedroom community of Seattle. Increasingly, it was where the money was—and my family didn't have any. Although the prosperity of the early sixties would eventually trickle down even to us, it hadn't yet. Living amid the affluence of Bellevue made our financial situation doubly hard.

That first year in Bellevue, we got a new television set for Christmas, and I discovered basketball. Every weekend, I would sit enthralled, watching the amazing on-court heroics of Russell and Chamberlain, "The Big O," and Jerry West. It has become a cliché, but in sports I saw a way to establish myself—a way to gain a social footing.

By the time I started ninth grade, I had decided to try out for the basketball team, even though I'd never played much. I spent several weeks lobbying my mother for the Converse All Stars and the doctor's physical that I needed to play (both were expensive, and unbudgeted). During tryouts, I was introduced to Paul Misuradze, who taught math and coached basketball at Tyee Junior High School.

It's been nearly four decades since that first tryout. I recall very little about that afternoon when twenty to thirty fourteen-year-old boys gathered in the school gym and began the series of drills and exercises that would determine my future. Our games, played every Friday night against other junior-high teams in our school district, are even more of a blur. What I do remember are the practices, which I dutifully attended every weekday for two to three hours after school. I don't believe I have ever applied myself to anything with such single-minded determination.

There were days when I was nearly crazed with the fear of failure, when I would curse myself for the most minuscule mistake. Shame would sweep over me whenever I'd let my man score or I'd throw the ball away. Every time I played at one of our games and a substitute would come in for me, I'd run to the sideline, head down, certain that I would never again be allowed onto the court. With each tiny misstep, I would feel less and less a part of the team and more and more isolated.

Paul Misuradze was the furthest thing from the popular depictions of coach as sadistic drill sergeant. About five-foot-eight, with coal-black hair and keenly intelligent eyes, Coach, as we all came to call him, was a soft-spoken, optimistic, and genuinely kind man who believed that in the beauty of basketball lay a pretty good model for life. (Today, when I coach my twelve-year-old son's youth-league team, it is Coach's vision of the game that guides me.) "Leavitt," he would say, taking me aside at practice on one of those days when I probably seemed about to implode, "you are tougher on yourself than the meanest, most cantankerous coach in the world could ever be." He'd lay a hand on my shoulder lightly, then add, "You're doing a great job. Just relax a little. If you keep working, everything will be all right."

It wasn't a profound message, but it was one that no one had ever bothered to impart. In today's jargon, I suppose, we'd say that Coach gave me self-esteem. Back then, all I knew was that when nobody else thought I was worth the effort, he took an interest in me and made me feel that I had something valuable to offer.

Gradually, I learned that I had an important place on the team. I wasn't much of a shooter. I couldn't dribble or pass. But I could play defense. So I became the defensive stopper. I discovered that if I worked hard for Coach, my game really would improve. Occasionally, I would hear him direct others to observe the way I performed a particular play and try to learn from me. He'd say, "Roy did a great job on that play" or "Watch Roy's moves—that's how the game is supposed to work." From the shared sense of a common goal with my teammates, a relaxed camaraderie arose among us, and that ease carried over to my life at school. As I walked down the long hallways, chatting casually with schoolmates, I felt for the first time that I truly belonged.

Having learned from Coach to value hard work, I started applying it everywhere. I focused on my schoolwork, and my grades skyrocketed. I began to think that perhaps I could go to college after all.

I have no idea how many games our team won or lost that year. But at season's end, I remember sitting in the gym during assembly and hearing my name called. Blushing at the loud, enthusiastic applause, I walked up to Coach, shook his hand, and accepted the trophy designating me the "Most Inspirational Player of the Year." I remember wishing with all my heart that we didn't have to move again.

But we did. The unthinkable was happening: my family's entry into the middle class was finally, if not in hand, at least within reach. True, my stepfather still worked two jobs, and my mother continued to clean motel rooms. But for the first time, they were about to become home owners, and our family was moving to a brand-new housing development in the neighboring town of Redmond. Which meant, of course, that once again I had to start at a different school in the middle of an academic year.

One evening that spring, when we'd been in our new house for about three months, my mother sent me out to the local Seven-Eleven to pick up a carton of milk. I took a shortcut through the woods behind our property—woods that, by the following spring, would be obliterated and parceled out for new homes. I walked into the store, grabbed the milk, and went to the check-out to pay. There, behind the counter, was Coach, working as the night clerk. I had one of those moments of cognitive dissonance that would become more and more familiar as I made my way in the world. Here was one of the most monumental, important people in my universe, and yet, I realized with a pang, he, like my stepfather, needed a second job in order to make ends meet. But at almost the same instant, as his face lit up with delight at seeing me, my initial sadness faded and was replaced with a sense of immutable kinship. After exchanging some sports small talk and a few more pleasantries, I said good-bye to Coach and left the store, my heart soaring.

That was the last time I saw him, but the impact he had on that unformed boy has reverberated down through the thirty-six years since that night. For better or worse, I stayed with basketball, playing on school teams throughout high school and on into college. Even now, at fifty (when, arguably, I should know better), I take part in a weekly pick-up game with a bunch of other middle-aged guys who refuse to accept that they're over the hill. I no longer have my youthful moves, but when I'm on the basketball court, I feel more at home than almost any place on earth.—*Roy Leavitt*

THANK YOU, MR. FELKER

Back in 1956, when I was twelve years old, my teacher, George Felker, saved my life—in more ways than one. Up until the time he rescued me, I'd loved my teachers but considered them my jailers because I was in a place I didn't want to be. Moreover, they were people I had to continually lie to. Mr. Felker pulled me out of this darkness into light.

I suffer from dyslexia, disnumeria, and disgraphia, which means I'm not able to read, understand numbers, or write in the usual ways. But when I was a child, these diagnoses didn't exist. All I knew was that there was something dreadfully, dreadfully wrong with me. And as a young girl, of course, I interpreted that something to be that I was dumb. It never occurred to me that I might have a perceptual difficulty and that there might be a name for it.

But even if my problem could have been diagnosed, I wouldn't have told anyone about it, especially my teachers. I wanted their love and respect so badly that I would rather have died than let them know the trouble I was in—which is bizarre, because they were the only ones who might have helped. Instead, I became an expert at covering up.

I tell you, I was adept. Even my mother, who was a teacher for thirty-eight years, suspected nothing. I fooled everyone through memorization. I'd hear my classmate read a paragraph and I'd stand up and literally recite the same thing, while holding a book in my hand. My teacher would just think I wasn't paying attention and had lost my place—not that I couldn't read the words.

In my case, all this was made even worse by the fact that I had a personal tormentor, a boy named Joey, who was in my class. He would wait for me in the schoolyard, then pin me against a wall, and say, "Hey, dumbbell, when are you going to get a clue? You're so ugly. Who dresses you?" He'd make fun of my hair, my teeth, my skin. There was nothing about me that he didn't absolutely crucify. And I believed everything he said. I missed school sometimes because it was so terrible. I'd have headaches and stomachaches; I even considered suicide. But, again, I never told a soul. Not only was I ashamed that it was happening to me, I also knew that if I reported him to anybody in authority, Joey would catch hell, and then he'd really let me have it. As horrible as it was, it would then have become murderous.

Such was the sorry state of my life when this glorious, elegant, handsome young man walked into our classroom. He was one of those spontaneous teachers far ahead of his time. He'd do things like incorporate the songs from Broadway musicals into our lessons. All of us, especially the girls in class, thought he was the greatest thing since sliced cheese. Naturally I had a crush on him.

One day he asked me to stay after school to help wash blackboards. This was an honor—to be asked to be alone with him and in his gaze, as it were. But of course he must have suspected something.

So Mr. Felker had me washing the blackboards to the accompaniment—aptly enough—of the *My Fair Lady* cast album. He asked me to make letters and numbers with the sponge, and at some point, I realized he was testing me. I remember he walked up to me, and I felt his hand in the center of my back. I can still feel it to this day.

I began to cry because I thought, "Now he's on to me—he knows I'm dumb." I figured I'd lost his friendship and admiration.

He sank to his knees and put his arm around my shoulder. "Oh, my God, you poor thing," he said. "The games you've had to play."

Then I really started to sob. "But I'm dumb," I wailed.

"How can you be dumb if you've fooled your teachers until your twelfth year? A dumb person can't do that." Then he said, "Look, I'm going to find you some help, because what you have, I believe, has a name. And I believe there are other people like you. You're not the only one." Remember, this was 1956. The man was a visionary.

He got what I assume was a reading specialist for me. Her name was Miss Plessy, and she came after school at least three days a week. Nobody ever said anything about paying her for her time, so I have concluded that Mr. Felker paid her out of his own pocket.

I don't remember a great deal about what they did, but I believe much of it was experimental. I remember they used tinted lenses, and I had to do a lot of movement, like dancing almost. (Movement is very important to kids who have learning disabilities.) I don't really know what part of the method worked—it could have been all of it—but suddenly one day it all clicked. I looked at a simple line of text and realized that it meant something. For the first time, I was understanding a cluster of words, and could pull up a mental image as I was looking at them! That was the breakthrough that allowed me to become a reader.

What Mr. Felker did is unthinkable now—that he'd stay alone with a twelve-year-old girl and that he'd touch me. Nowadays, teachers aren't allowed to touch their students in any way. And that's so regrettable—some of the hugs I got from teachers changed my life.

But Mr. Felker also helped me in another way that could never happen today: he pulled Joey off me, and that whole miserable chapter of my life simply disappeared. I was hiding under the stairs so I wouldn't have to go outside (it was a requirement) because Joey's favorite place to attack me was in the schoolyard. Mr. Felker caught Joey in the act of tormenting me. I'll never forget how he literally picked that boy up by his shirt and dragged him to the principal's office. These days you'd probably get sued for doing that. But in this case, believe me, such intervention was necessary. After that, Joey never came back to our school again. So obviously I wasn't his only victim.

My family moved away from that California town a couple of years later, but I saw Mr. Felker again about eight years ago, when I was back in California for the wedding of a mutual acquaintance. I recognized him immediately, and at the reception I walked over and said, "Mr. Felker, you may not remember me, but I want you to know what you did for me." I recounted the whole story and mentioned that I had become a children's book author. Both of us wound up weeping.

In 1998, when I was writing my book about him, *Thank You, Mr. Falker* (I made the main character, Trisha, younger than I was because it is a picture book), I tried to contact George Felker, searching on all the Web sites and getting in touch with the California Teachers Association and looking every other place I could think of. But his name was nowhere to be found. The book is my way of paying homage to him and all the other Mr. Felkers out there. As I say in its dedication, he will forever be my hero.—*Patricia Polacco*

AUTOGRAPH

Thick, satin smooth, edged with gold,
The pages were pastel background prisms for
the words of my grammar school classmates.

In the spirit of school's last days, they scribbled
typical drawings, rhymes of our age. "When you
get married and have twins, don't come to my house

for safety pins." We thought them uproarious.
When I handed the precious blue book
to my teacher, she wrote, in elegant script,

"She walks in gentleness." I mumbled thanks,
walked back to my desk. Corners frayed, it lies
atop a box of memory scraps I cannot throw away.

A four-word map to remind me when I think
no one sees or hears or cares: One day, someone
paused long enough to peer into my heart.

—*Diana Rosen*

MORE RIGHT THAN WRONG

Miss Vivian Costen was an old-maid school teacher, and somehow she took a liking to me and I to her. I'd go to her every time I had a problem. She was like a mother to me. She left the school soon after I did. She died a little less than a year before I won the Heavyweight title. It was a great loss to me.

Miss Costen gave me confidence in myself. She made me feel I was important. She could tell that I was impressionable and a great sufferer. She knew that I was hurt by a raised voice. She wouldn't accept my protests that I couldn't learn to read or write. She was so kind and considerate and understanding that I wanted more than anything else in the world to please her. She bought me clothes and gave me little gifts. I had to return that to her in some way, and the only way I knew— or was able to—was to be what she wanted me to be.

I imagine I was a little slow, even with her patience, because in the classroom when she'd ask a question I still didn't dare raise my hand to answer. One day she asked a question of all the kids. She went around the room asking this one and that one. Everybody answered but me. I said I didn't know the answer. Then she told us the answer. Everybody in the class had been wrong, but the answer I had in my mind was correct, and I had not had nerve enough to say it out loud.

That made me furious. I just stood up and ran right out of that room. I could hear footsteps after me, but I didn't care. It was Miss Costen. She took me by the shoulders and lifted my head to look into my eyes. There were tears of shame and anger in them.

"I knew you knew the answer, Floyd," she said. "That's why you're crying. This should prove to you that if you have an idea, speak it out."

"I was afraid I'd sound stupid and everybody would laugh," I said.

Miss Costen put her arms around me and said, "Always remember this, Floyd Patterson. You're not stupid. You're the same as any other boy your own age. From now on I want you to answer. If you're wrong, you're wrong. Nobody's always right, but you'll be right more often than you're wrong."

Well, after that I sort of woke up. I began answering questions. I wasn't right more often than I was wrong. It was the other way at first, but gradually I was right 50 percent of the time, then 60 percent. I got to the point where I began to grasp the thing. I felt equal to the other boys. I didn't feel anymore that I had to sit there like an idiot, knowing nothing, saying nothing, and caring about nothing.—*Floyd Patterson*

THE ART OF AUTOBIOGRAPHY

I stormed into the classroom like a well-trained cutthroat, sliding in front of a blind woman with a cane who was walking too slowly. My speech was muddled, my movements frantic. I spotted a petite blond woman standing at the head of four tables pushed together seminar-style. She seemed as young as a graduate student and looked like Cybill Shepherd—a radical departure from the white-haired (and male) engineering professors I was accustomed to—but she was holding an attendance roster. So I rushed up to her and barked, "Can I take your class?"

I had no business being there. This was Contemporary Women's Autobiography, a writing and literature class for Ph.D. candidates at the University of Iowa. My undergraduate degree was in mechanical engineering, and I had recently finished a management training program for a large food manufacturing company. Yet here I was, demanding a spot in a graduate-level English course to which I hadn't even bothered to apply. And Dr. Patricia Foster let me in.

There, in that welcoming classroom, she and the rest of the women writers listened attentively to my autobiography. As I shared my stories of growing up as an Asian immigrant and of my struggles in the white, male-dominated culture of corporate America, they in turn recounted the abortions they'd had as teenagers, the husbands and children they'd left behind to pursue graduate school, the religious cults they'd been dragged to by their mothers. We entrusted secrets to one another that some of us had never divulged to our closest friends.

The blind woman I had nearly mowed down that first day described the tragic details of how she had lost her sight. I wept when I heard her story—partially in sympathy and partially at the realization of how horribly cold I had become. My attempt to cut past her to gain some slight, momentary advantage was all too characteristic of the callousness that was now second-nature to me.

My grammar was horrifying and my word choices clumsy, but Professor Foster helped me get my language skills back in shape after years of austere math calculations and somber physics formulas. I found myself possessed by an urgency to write, and she made me feel that I had the tools to express my innermost thoughts and feelings. She let me rant when I was full of myself for making a lot of money, yet she never wavered in her own dignity. In the work world, I had been trained to intimidate in order to establish my credibility. In Professor Foster's classroom, I discovered not only that these tactics were useless but also how dearly they had cost me.

She led the class in accepting me, the oddball non-graduate student, and helped reawaken my true self, the one that kept poking its head out from under its shell like a giant sea turtle gasping for air. The stories I told and wrote seemed always to be about my family, and it became clear that I had to return to my roots to lay to rest the ghosts that were handcuffing me to my past.

At the end of the semester, as the class drew to a close, I made the decision to drop out of the frantic chase for more and more money and a better and better career—priorities programmed into many immigrants from an early age. I quit my job and returned to my family in New Jersey, enrolling in a nearby Master's of Liberal Arts program.

It was Professor Foster who ushered me over that threshold. At a point when I had reached terminal velocity in my scramble to the top of the conformity ladder, she gave me the confidence to stop. I doubt she has any idea how crucial she was in helping me break free of the stranglehold of the American immigrant's dream of material success. With a grip that never wavered, she held a mirror up to my soul—and in doing so, she restored my humanity.—*Helen i-lin Hwang*

POPE GEORGE THE FIRST

"Reverent, kind, and extremely interested in all his students." That's how a recent article in my high school's alumni magazine characterized its former headmaster, George A. Walton, who served from 1912 to 1948. The article went on to say, "One colleague described him as tender toward the bashful, gentle toward the distant, and merciful toward the absurd." Accurate adjectives all—and he was a progressive thinker as well. It was George Walton, I remembered, who invited the prominent African-American leader Walter White, secretary of the NAACP, to visit our school for several days back in the early forties, and Walton who singled me out to be White's host.

Reading about Walton made me wonder how many other students over the years had been similarly touched and inspired by this extraordinary educator. A flood of memories came rushing back from more than half a century ago—including one I cherish above all others.

I entered George School, a coeducational Quaker boarding school in Newtown, Pennsylvania, in spring 1943, midway through my junior year. The yearbook described me as a "philosopher, inventor, and expert knife and axe thrower." In hindsight, I'd say I was bored with most of my schoolwork but passionate (to a fault) about my inventions.

More often that not, it was my roommate, Wally, who suggested the projects and I who put them into practice. For example, we slept with our window wide open, and even though the steam heat came hissing and burbling from the radiator well before dawn, Wally complained about having to get up in a near-freezing room. (Why, you ask, did we not simply close the window at night before we went to sleep, or open it just a crack? I've wondered the same thing myself all these years.) I obliged by building a window closer—an elaborate, multi-faceted contraption that would have put Rube Goldberg to shame. It was my dubious ingenuity that got us into trouble.

First, I ballasted the double-hung window sash with a gallon bottle of water, to overcome the sash weights. Then I fashioned a release mechanism—a nail passed through two screw eyes with a string looped around—that held up the window during the night. When the power went on again in the morning, a 6-volt bell transformer (hidden in my oak foot locker under the window) activated a 6-volt doorbell, which in turn released the pad of a mousetrap, jerking the nail free, thus breaking the electrical circuit and releasing the window sash to close by gravity.

When first bell woke us—in our toasty-warm room—to get ready for breakfast, we packed the whole contraption up and hid the electrical parts in the padlocked locker, away from prying eyes. Or so we thought. We were quite delighted, even a little smug, with our success. However, we had failed to reckon with Mr. Sutton, the sharp-eyed athletic director who lived with his sharp-eared wife in an apartment directly below our room. Needless to say, we were found out.

Shortly thereafter, I was called to appear before the headmaster, George A. Walton, in his office. Mr. Walton was tall, bony, and balding. He was not only the secular Head of School but also its spiritual guide. Hence, I assume, his nickname "The Pope." Although Mr. Walton was very erect and dignified, his face always carried a kindly expression, and he was never brusque or in a hurry. He was, in short, that rarest of creatures: a genuinely good man.

When I entered the Pope's office, I knew I was to be disciplined. Yet I also sensed this would be very different from my prior experience at the hands (and, alas, the cane) of Mr. Conrad, the headmaster at my very proper English prep school. Sensitive soul that he was, George Walton must have observed that my self-esteem had been damaged as a child— I could not look my teachers in the eye—for he seemed to bind old wounds. As I walked in, he invited me to close the door and sit down. After a pause to let me feel at home, he leaned back in his chair, relaxed and smiling. "John," he said, "I must tell you how much I admire you. I wish I had the creativity, skill, and inventiveness that you have demonstrated. Please allow me to congratulate you."

I could scarcely believe my ears, but his sincerity was unmistakable. Watching me carefully and letting his words settle in, he went on. "I trust you," he said, "and I have been assured by the school's mechanics that your invention was perfectly safe and constituted no danger to anyone." He sighed heavily. "However, rules are for everyone's protection, and unfortunately it is my responsibility to enforce them. Therefore, I regret that I must give you one demerit."

As I left his office, I felt lifted up. Instead of being punished, I had been recognized. Instead of being shamed or banished, I had been acknowledged and accepted. The gift I received in those few moments with Pope George A. Walton has stayed with me my entire life.
— *John Fisher-Smith*

A BRIGHT SPOT IN A DARK LANDSCAPE

Nowadays, the fifties are viewed through the friendly haze of nostalgia, but people forget (or never knew, because they're too young) how deadly that era was. And the New Jersey suburb where my family lived in the 1950s—anointed by a national magazine as "the typical American town"—was one of the most stifling places on earth. If you were different in any way, you were a pariah. For me, being overweight was the difference on which I hung all my problems and insecurities.

At my junior high and high school, there was a pecking order of cliques, and I was at the bottom. In a place where not looking like Doris Day was impermissible, I was the fat girl who was unpopular. I wasn't cute, and I wasn't the least bit perky. I looked ludicrous in a cashmere twin set. I was the antiDoris Day: sullen, angry, miserable, and . . . fat. (As it turned out, Doris Day wasn't so happy at the time either, but who knew? We were all expert dissemblers.) I never had a date. I did have a few friends, but I didn't actually like them much. They were the only kids who would talk to me, so I was stuck with them.

In addition to my lowly social status, I also felt stupid, because I never got any encouragement from teachers. Except in Mr. Stanton's class. He made me feel—and I think he made an effort to make me feel—that I was bright and had something to say. That I was special. Outrageous, maybe, but special. The other teachers would just correct my grammar and punctuation and give me a C. He gave me good grades and paid attention to my ideas.

I'm not even sure if I had Mr. Stanton in eighth or ninth grade—this period was so painful I've blocked most of it out—but I do remember the breast moment.

We were supposed to write a report on a poem, and I chose D. H. Lawrence's poem about breasts. I was very taken with Lawrence (the feminist movement hadn't yet been invented, so he hadn't yet been denounced as a chauvinist pig) because the unbridled sexuality and sensuality of his writing were so antithetical to the spirit of the times. He just totally flipped me out. What can I say? I wasn't a fifties person.

I probably wrote something very sophomoric and silly and sentimental. Mr. Stanton pretended to be shocked: "Oh! Norma! How could you? What a scandal!" And he laughed and seemed to think I was clever. You have to understand how unprecedented this sort of recognition was: no other teacher had ever shown any appreciation for my intelligence or even seemed to think I had any. Mr. Stanton clearly got a kick out of my attempts to be risqué.

School didn't suddenly get better after that, but his class was a tiny bright spot in a very dark landscape. He liked me and encouraged me, and that was enough.

Mr. Stanton looked a little like Ichabod Crane—very tall and skinny, and he always dressed in black. He wore suits, because teachers always wore suits. And he must have had something approximating a crew cut, or he wouldn't have been allowed to teach. I recall now that he moved in a somewhat effeminate way, though that meant nothing to me at the time.

I guess I realized he was gay when I was in my twenties and ran into some people from my old high school who, it turned out, were gay themselves. That's when I thought back. Evidently, there had been people at my school who'd been deep, deep in the closet, yet I hadn't even known there was a closet. I had never heard of homosexuality. That's how repressed this era was. In a time and place where difference was a disease, Mr. Stanton and I were fellow sufferers. I'd never recognized that, but on some level, I saw now, he had.

Once I understood about Mr. Stanton, I realized that three of the four other teachers I related to had all been gay men. The fourth was in a wheelchair. We were all misfits. That was our bond. And my salvation.—*Norma Katzman*

THE CIRCLE OF LOVE

Every morning, Mrs. Anna Voss's gentle blue eyes met mine, and her face lit up in a way that told me how much she loved me. She kissed my dirty little five-year-old face and kept me warm with her gentle hugs. It didn't take long for me to figure out that I was her pet. Of course, I now realize that every other first-grader felt exactly the same way.

"What is the letter? D, yes, that's right. What is the next letter?" And then the lavish praise. "You are so smart and so pretty."

The youngest of five children, I didn't get a whole lot of praise at home. I couldn't make the beds or dress anybody else. I couldn't even reach the dishpan to wash the dishes. But I had beautiful golden curls that shone like a halo around my timid little soul. And Mrs. Voss never once let me forget how special they were.

She taught in a two-room schoolhouse that was heated by a little pot-belly stove. She could watch the boys from the upper grades who kept our stove fueled—they had to chop the wood and build the fires—while switching adeptly back and forth from the topic at hand. She taught us math, English, spelling, science, reading, writing, and health in this way. And by her gentleness, she instilled in us social skills that would last a lifetime.

One morning, I arrived at school hanging my head. My older sister, perhaps jealous of my halo, had "accidentally" sheared my hair to a quarter of an inch all over my head. The glorious curls that turned heads in my direction were gone. Even Mrs. Voss, momentarily stunned, asked, "Rosie, what happened to your hair?" For just a moment, there was no sunshine in her smile.

I tried frantically to explain. "Her scissors slipped," I began, and then I simply wept.

Mrs. Voss made a smooth and instant recovery. "It will grow and be beautiful. You'll see. And you will be smarter and prettier than ever." The circle of her arms was warmer than the pot-belly stove. Since that day, my goal has been to learn to show love her way, openly and honestly, especially in hard times.—*Rose Martin*

MAKING THE CONNECTION

We moved to Cold Spring Harbor the summer before my sophomore year in high school. I had gone to a private country day school since kindergarten, and I was really excited about attending my first public high school and the vast social opportunities that represented. A class of a hundred kids seemed huge after spending ten years with the same eighteen classmates at Woodmere Academy.

I'd just experienced the Long Island Jewish girl's version of ritual circumcision—Dr. Silver's patented Five-Towns nose job ("not that she really needed it," my mother would say for years afterward) and I was determined to reinvent myself as a way cooler individual than I'd been in my old school. My new persona was a guitar-playing, poetry-writing, political-activist, lefty folksinger. Imagine a baby Joan Baez. No one had to know that at my old school I had been a geeky, painfully shy social misfit.

I was not prepared for the academic disparity between private and public school, and after a boring month in a regular tenth-grade English class, I requested a transfer to Honors English. And suddenly, I was challenged and excited in a way I have never been before or since.

Alan Grossman's genius as a teacher was in training us to look beneath the surface for underlying themes and connections. At the same time, he showed us how differences of race, gender, income, and age were superficial. This may not sound like earth-shattering news in today's multicultural, inclusive society, but at that time in my life, it was a spine-tingling revelation. His insights and intellect floated around the room, waiting to be grabbed and devoured by precocious young poetry-writing high school girls like me.

The day that had the greatest impact was November 22, 1963, the day JFK was shot. The announcement came over the loudspeaker, and in the stunned silence that followed Mr. Grossman placed a poetry anthology on each of our desks and asked us to turn to the Walt Whitman poem, "When Lilacs Last in the Dooryard Bloom'd":

When lilacs last in the dooryard bloom'd,
And the great star droop'd in the western sky in the night,
I mourn'd and yet shall mourn with ever-returning spring.
Ever-returning spring, trinity sure to me you bring,
Lilac blooming perennial and drooping star in the west,
And thought of him I love.

O powerful fallen western star!
O shades of night—O moody tearful night!
O great star disappear'd—O the black murk that hides the star!
O cruel hands that hold me powerless—O helpless soul of me!
O harsh surrounding cloud that will not free my soul.

Mr. Grossman was calm and subdued, and, as usual, in an instant had come up with the perfect—the only—appropriate response to such appalling news. I was always grateful for the timing. Had it happened one hour earlier, I would have been in history class, where that teacher's weepy hand-wringing would have been hard to stomach.

Mr. Grossman was—and is—a lifelong Homer scholar. His insights into the *Iliad* and the *Odyssey* (not to mention Shakespeare, John

Barth, Tom Stoppard, Albert Camus, and countless others) were, in the slang of the times, mindblowing, and the reading we did in his classes turned my entire life around. I'd always loved books, but his ability to make connections between myth, literature, archetype, psychology, poetry, and philosophy made me see the world, and everything I read forever after, in a different light.

In class, Mr. Grossman's manner was somewhat abrupt and impatient, but he worked diligently to get us to think beyond our safety zone. It was sometimes hard to keep up when our material went beyond our personal experience. We were mystified, for example, by the reference to sexual positions in John Barth's *Giles Goat-Boy*.

By twelfth grade (when I was again taught by Mr. Grossman), I wasn't a new kid anymore and had basically established my image to the point where everyone, including me, believed it. I was performing a lot in folk-music clubs and at hootenannies. I put together a series of folk-music shows in the park during the summer with a couple of friends. I volunteered at the local Freedom Center, teaching underprivileged kids from Huntington Station how to read. But mostly, I spent every spare moment in New York City, sleeping on my older cousin's sofa in Greenwich Village and sitting in cafes on MacDougal Street for hours on end, between trips to the Folklore Center to buy strings and guitar picks and the latest issue of *Sing Out* magazine. I would hang out all day in the Village, then go home and breathlessly write in my diary about having played checkers with a "real existentialist."

So this other life—and the fact I'd been accepted on early decision to Antioch College—made school seem pretty useless and stupid. But one saving grace was the generosity and friendship extended by Mr. Grossman and his wife, Jean. An accomplished musician, Jean joined him in opening their home to a select group of his favorite students on many weekend afternoons that senior year. It was an ordinary suburban house with a small yard, but what was extraordinary was that it was filled with music at all times. Their daughter, Spring, played violin, and their twin sons, Sam and Irving, played trumpet.

We barbecued burgers, read our mostly very bad poetry, heard marvelous stories about the Grossmans' adventures in Paris, and listened to the latest Dave Brubeck LPs. There were four of us girls who published the high-school literary magazine and pretty much had the run of the English department. Being treated with respect and as good thinkers (things were so different for girls in the sixties—take my word for it) was as heady and intoxicating as the cheap Chianti we could sometimes get away with ordering in Greenwich Village dives.

For some reason, we never gave much thought to the fact that an overworked teacher was extending himself to the point of giving up his weekends to entertain us. But we never turned down an invitation! Of course Alan Grossman seemed old to us then. After all, he was a grown-up, married with young children, living in suburbia, and teaching high school. I realize in retrospect that he was barely thirty—a bohemian with a day job. But if Mr. Grossman appeared bourgeois, Jean was exotic—extremely thin when Twiggy was the rage, and light-years ahead of the watered-down Jackie Kennedy look favored by other suburban wives. As fledgling hippie girls desperate for an alternative role model, we adored her.

I went to Antioch as planned. I thought about Mr. Grossman a lot during college, where I earned an interdisciplinary philosophy and psychology degree in 1971. The background I gained from his classes gave me a jump on that material. After graduation, a radio job brought me to San Francisco, where I now own a literary media escort company. Basically, I baby-sit authors who come through town on book tours.

Over the years, I've kept in loose touch with Alan Grossman. I've gotten a kick out of being able to share stories with him about my adventures with some of his literary heroes, and I've recommended books for him to read. Up until Jean's losing bout with breast cancer a few years ago, Alan was still teaching at my old school. Last year, I paid him a visit. He had retired when Jean became ill and was still actively grieving, but he asked for a reading list of some of my favorite new authors. He finds it entertaining that I'm friends with Norman Mailer or have had midnight supper with Gore Vidal. I find it thrilling that I'm finally able to reciprocate for the stories about Paris and his kind ear toward our bad poetry.—*Kathi Kamen Goldmark*

LIVING UP TO EXPECTATIONS

I was only a few months past my eleventh birthday when I entered Mrs. Sylvia Carlin's seventh-grade English class in my extremely poor Brooklyn neighborhood, but I looked so much as if I belonged in high school that I felt embarrassed about being there. I was the tallest child in the class, and the frequency and vehemence with which my mother and a cabal of other relatives ordered me to stop growing had failed to build up any psychological immunity. In addition, Momma's obvious delight in telling me that I was an accident was an ego-depleter for which even my history of success in school could not compensate.

In the scheme of things, I felt painfully superfluous.

In this private desert, where I had serious doubts that I could ever bloom, Mrs. Carlin was a refreshing rain shower. She lavished extravagant praise on everything I did. She told Momma that I had outstanding ability in English, and she gave me grades of 100 on my report card. These accolades gave me no illusions of perfection, but they did wonders for my sense of self-worth.

At the end of the school year, Mrs. Carlin got a teaching position in a Manhattan high school and left my Brooklyn junior high. I bought an autograph album so I could have a written memento of her. What she wrote I treasured enough to commit to memory: "Don't disappoint us, Louise. We expect you to be the author of a best-seller."

I took her prediction as both magical prophecy and obligation. Largely because of her encouragement and validation at a time when I was so ravenous for them, I took and passed the difficult entrance examination for Hunter College High School. Graduating from this demanding academic institution set off a chain reaction that ended with a doctorate in English, received a few months before my twenty-ninth birthday. After a long teaching career at the City University of New York, I retired as a Professor of English in 1995.

For many years I had longed to phone Mrs. Carlin, who the phone directory told me still lived in Brooklyn, and let her know what I had become. But I hesitated, remembering what she had written in my album and fearing my lack of literary acclaim would disappoint her. Or worse, I realized, she might not even remember me. Roughly thirty-four years from the time I first entered her classroom, I worked up the courage to make that call. She remembered me immediately. We arranged to meet for lunch, had no trouble recognizing each other, and have been close friends ever since. When frustrations revive my youthful hunger for validation and reassurance, Mrs. Carlin is still there to remind me that once an eleven-year-old was outstanding enough to imprint herself on a teacher's memory.—*Louise Jaffe*

TRUE TO MY SCHOOL

Daughter of a peripatetic rabbi, I was used to stealth school attendance: we'd move into a town, and I'd register at the local schools, attend for a while, then leave to relocate to some other place more in keeping with my father's impossible standards.

In six years, we logged seven moves. As the New Girl in class, I was forever being scrutinized. And there was plenty about me that was different. My name: Marion with an *o*, not an *a*. My funny British accent. My ambiguous academic background. All were fair game for the thirty-plus kids who already knew one another but never me.

The schools fell on a continuum from tough and rigorous in my native Manchester, England, to scholastically relaxed in Columbus, Ohio. I never worried about missing parts of the curriculum or about playing catch-up, since my parents had been supplementing my formal education with home schooling from the time I was a small child.

What I did lack—apart from stability—was a sense of my standing relative to my classmates. Although I always managed to get top grades, I was never told I was doing a good job or encouraged to do a better one. Until, that is, I enrolled in Dr. Applebaum's English class.

The word was out on Dr. A: one tough teacher. Solidly built, impeccably dressed, and coldly supercilious, he terrified the entire ninth grade at Central High School for Girls in New York City. At our first dressing-down—on the fifth day of class, he chastised us for sloppy syntax, diction, and grammar in our compositions on the poetry of John Masefield—he selected one essay as exemplary. As he began reading it aloud, we didn't know whether it exemplified the worst or the best of the lot—or was just one typically wretched essay among many. As I listened, I at first reacted in wonderment that someone else styled her sentences exactly as I did. After two paragraphs, I blushed crimson. But Dr. A wasn't ridiculing the theme—he was exalting it. He praised my word usage, my choice of topic, the sophistication of my sentence structure. I sat there in disbelief. Had there been a mix-up?

Although my essay had not been an especially heroic effort, it was the first time I'd ever been singled out and publicly commended for my creative output. (Not that I got a lot of private recognition, either: My parents, with typical British reserve, had little to say about grades or schoolwork.) Dr. A's praise—my first taste of sugar—sent me soaring. I began writing like mad. Poetry. Comic strips. Intricately plotted short stories. Rudimentary newsletters that I distributed on the beach. Catalogs of jokes that I submitted to magazines. Obsessively detailed journal entries. Long, chatty letters to faraway pen pals.

Shortly after that day, at Dr. A's urging, I entered and won a city-wide essay contest on that old war-horse of topics—becoming a naturalized American citizen. A few months later, again encouraged by Dr. A, I won an award for my poetry. Most gratifying of all, I finally began to feel that I belonged somewhere. For the first (and, indeed, the only) time in my life, I positively bubbled with school spirit. The capper to that "rebirthing" year was when I submitted a geography question I had puzzled over to a local newspaper contest and placed first. I don't believe I have ever felt prouder of a prize: an entire, brand-new set of the Encyclopedia Britannica for my high-school library.—*Marion DS Dreyfus*

FLYING WITHOUT A RUDDER

Miss Mable Malloy—a petite, gray-haired woman in British woolen skirts, silk blouses, and brooches, with penetrating eyes magnified by crystal-clear wire framed glasses—has been my constant inspiration. She gave me hope during my most difficult days.

I was born Eugene John Douthit on February 8, 1932, in San Francisco General Hospital. My early life was marked by massive disruptions—my father deserted us, and after my grandmother died, my mother, four older siblings, and I shuttled from place to place, from school to school, living on welfare.

We were desperately poor, and I was subjected to constant humiliation. Girls would say things like, "I don't want to sit in front of you because you have old shoes and I can smell them." Because we were so poor, I received a free lunch—a fact that the PTA volunteers would invariably advertise by shouting across the cafeteria, "Does he have a free lunch?" I had no friends. My mother, who was like a child herself, didn't allow me to have any visitors at home.

My sisters had taught me how to read before I went to school, and I picked up math on my own. But my handwriting was atrocious, in a school where the teachers were handwriting freaks, so they constantly hit me with a ruler for my lack of achievement.

After one particularly harrowing incident with a principal at one of the many schools I attended, I remained at home in the garage for three days, contemplating suicide by swallowing Drano. My mother did not challenge the principal's action, for her own tragic personal reasons: She had no proper clothes to wear to school and to come in her rags would have been too humiliating. I was really suicidal.

In seventh grade, my mother and sisters and I lived in one room over a Chinese laundry. It was chaos. I enrolled in Marina Junior High School and immediately got into trouble with the gym teacher because I didn't have the required outfit. That particular garment wasn't available at the Goodwill Store where we bought almost everything we wore.

Then, as punishment for talking in class, the science teacher ordered me to wash the front stairs of the school. I refused—the punishment did not fit the crime—and I was suspended for two weeks. I had seen the Fredric March film version of *Les Misérables* when I was nine, and I felt like Jean Valjean: nineteen years in chains for stealing a loaf of bread. (In 1990, I officially changed my last name to Valjean.)

During my suspension, I went downtown to the San Francisco School District office, where an administrator who heard my story arranged for me to meet the principal of Grant School, one of the city's best. The principal spelled out behavioral conditions I could easily handle and arranged an early-morning meeting with Miss Mable Malloy.

Miss Malloy reviewed the rules with me, and then took me upstairs to her room, gave me books, supplies, and copies of the most recent student lessons and assigned me a seat. When the class came in from the schoolyard, Miss Malloy introduced me to the other kids, assigning a couple of them to show me around. She never talked about where I'd come from or how I got there. She just said I was a new student who had transferred in. For the first time in my life, I felt I was an asset to the class. I had never before felt anything but a burden. Eugene the Reject was suddenly acceptable.

Miss Malloy saw to it that I had a free lunch each day, but with no fanfare. Sometimes that lunch was my only meal. More than that, she asked me how I felt about things. She talked to me. When helping students with their work, she would always add a gentle recommendation for perfecting it. And she had this wonderful technique for helping us improve without making us feel like we needed improvement. She'd say "That's looking great—what do you think of this?" I had never before been able to do anything right for a teacher.

She also possessed a trait that all master teachers seem to share: the art of theater. She breathed life into the great inventors, artists, writers, musicians, scientists, and literary characters we studied. In her class we acted out the assassination of Julius Caesar with wooden knives and togas made of sheets and ropes. She provided tickets to the San Francisco Symphony for me and another poor student, and I fell in love with classical music. I still don't know where she got those tickets. Somehow, too, I magically received clothing to wear to the concerts: an anonymous donor sent a beautiful—albeit used—navy blue blazer and necktie, and a new white shirt.

And we learned. She encouraged us to seek out experts for information, so when I had to give a report on Alcatraz, I wrote to the warden, Salt Water Johnson, who sent me information about the prison (though he did not allow the requested first-hand visit). She also invited guests to speak to the class. General Stilwell spoke about his efforts in Burma during World War II, and Glenn Seaborg, the nuclear chemist, came to talk to our class. We learned about astronomy, atomic fission, half-life, watercolor technique, literature, Roman and Greek culture, and a bit of Latin and Greek. (Her philosophy dictated that to be a cultured person, you must study Greek.) We even learned some Hebrew from the Jewish kids in class. Through it all, my penmanship was still hopeless, almost unreadable, but the marvelous Miss Malloy read and corrected my outrageous graffiti with patience and care.

We learned about telescopes, too—the remarkable 200-inch project at Mt. Palomar and the 100-inch at Lick Observatory in the mountains above San Jose. For a while, I wanted to be an astronomer until I realized that I would have to live on an isolated mountaintop—no place for a city boy. Miss Malloy had seen Halley's Comet around 1910, and she ecstatically shared her experience. "If you live long enough," she said, "you'll be able to see it too." She made the planets, the stars, and our place in the universe palpable to us.

It was an altogether wonderful eighth-grade year. With Miss Malloy, I made a complete turnaround as a student. I had been flying without a rudder, and she gave me one. She kept saying, "Eugene, you're going to do well." And suddenly, I could go in any direction I chose. Until then, I'd always assumed I'd just be a laborer somewhere. Of my four older siblings, three had already become high-school dropouts. Now I began to think of going beyond high school.

And I did. I joined the Air Force, where I taught radar, and when I came out of the service, I started college, eventually earning a degree in economics from the University of San Francisco. But that was only the beginning of a lifetime of learning and teaching. In 1965, as one of eleven national winners of the Goethe Institute Scholarship Competition sponsored by the West German government, I spent a summer studying German in Bad Reichenhall, Bavaria, near Salzburg, Austria, and in 1985 I won a Fulbright Fellowship for eight weeks of study in The People's Republic of China.

I was a high school teacher for fourteen years and a principal for twenty-five. Through it all, my role model was Miss Malloy. To my everlasting regret, I never returned to tell her how much she meant to me. But if I could speak to her today, I would tell her that she was the greatest teacher I've ever known. I would tell her that my life was utterly changed because of her. I had never thought of college, or of my future—indeed, I had no future. Without her, I would have ended up unloading boxes on a dock someplace, if I hadn't died first.

Miss Malloy is never far from my mind. Every time there's an eclipse, I think of her. When I play the French horn, I remember how she taught me to love music. When I paint, I recall the time I won the citywide art competition under her guidance. And in 1986, when I viewed Halley's Comet from Goldendale, Washington, on a twenty-inch telescope, Miss Malloy was at my side. As she has been for every one of my triumphs, large and small.—*Eugene Valjean*

CHAPTER SIX

Will This Be On the Test?

Listening to young people talk about their education can be a demoralizing proposition. "What did you get in Gradgrind's class?" one asks. "I aced that test," boasts another. Yet another simply goes online to Term Papers R Us and downloads a research project on the English Restoration. A teacher pauses in the midst of explicating a particularly tortuous problem to ask if there are any questions, and the hands shoot up: "Will this be on the test?" Face it: in today's bottom-line culture, it is not an altogether unreasonable query.

Sometimes, though, if we're lucky, a teacher comes along who pushes aside such narrow concerns as test scores, GPAs, or getting into the right college. This teacher invites us to discover the deeper satisfactions at the heart of true learning—an often difficult process that carries peculiar rewards that have nothing whatsoever to do with arriving at a letter from A to F, or a number from 0 to 100. What defines such teachers is usually a combination of passion and mastery, coupled with an unshakable faith that their mission as educators is to inspire the same passion and mastery in us. So when we are in their classrooms, we no longer scribble frantically, straining to capture every word they utter (should we be required to regurgitate it on the final). Instead—to invoke the memorable phrase of Stanley Bulley, a college music-appreciation professor remembered in this chapter—we simply "put down our pens and listen!"

IF AT FIRST...

I was a scatter-brained adolescent when I enrolled in Miss Leavitt's first-year Latin class. Steeped as I was in romantic poetry, I figured a dead language was as far from harsh reality as one could possibly get and, therefore, right up my alley.

Miss Leavitt fascinated me from the start. All the adult women I knew made some concessions to fashion, no matter how puny or mis-guided. They plucked their eyebrows into fine lines, applied circles of hot-pink rouge to their cheeks, frizzed their hair with permanent waves. Not Miss Leavitt. No color tinged her long, pale face. No mascara brightened the eyes that crowded close to the narrow, patrician nose. No errant lock escaped the iron-gray bun. The sole ornament decorating the navy-blue or black dresses she wore was the pince-nez that hung from a black ribbon over her bony chest.

She would sit at her desk like a judge on his bench, never attempting to entertain or to win us over. Occasionally, she would give a short lecture on ancient Roman civilization, suggesting with her dry delivery that the decision whether to listen was entirely up to us. It was as if she possessed a body of knowledge so valuable in itself that she had no need for any of the usual attention-getting devices.

Class involved a daily vocabulary quiz and a weekly grammar and translation test. I got a 100 on the first weekly test—nouns of the first declension—though I had not the vaguest notion what "declension" meant. (Several crucial years of my elementary education had been spent at a progressive school where the learning of basic grammar was considered passé.) By the time we reached the second declension, I was hopelessly lost.

Several times a week, I would stay after school while Miss Leavitt patiently reviewed the tests and quizzes I had failed. Her brown eyes would regard me quizzically, as if she couldn't believe my ineptitude was genuine. Her expression, strangely enough, never upset or discouraged me. I was determined simply to learn what she had to teach. Unfortunately, I utterly lacked the tools. I failed first-year Latin.

"Why do you bother?" my mother asked as she scanned my final report card. "You don't need Latin."

Rebellious teenager that I was, I probably would have dropped Latin immediately if my mother had told me how important it was. Instead, I took it over in summer school and enrolled in second-year Latin the following autumn.

If Miss Leavitt was distressed to see me back in her class, she never showed it. About halfway through the year, my understanding of grammar began to improve, and I found Caesar's *Commentaries* relatively easy to translate. (He always seemed to be pitching camp, crossing a river, or planning a march.) My downfall that year was my general sloppiness and poor study skills (more fallout from my progressive elementary school). I was content to approximate a translation and rarely bothered to make sure that verbs agreed with their subjects.

Again that second year, Miss Leavitt kept me after school on a regular basis. I began to sense a growing intimacy between us—as if we had become allies in an all-out campaign to conquer Latin. Slowly, the red checks on my test papers became more scarce. The C+ I earned at the end of the year filled me with hope.

Latin III was a time of great awakening. Gradually, order began to assert itself over the chaos in my mind. I developed study techniques, learned to check my own work, mastered participles, and came to terms with "contingency" and "contrary to fact" in the subjunctive mood.

The skills I acquired in Miss Leavitt's class carried over to my other subjects, improving my grades in English, French, science, and history. More important, I discovered the true joy of learning—the satisfaction that comes from mastering a difficult subject and that has nothing whatsoever to do with grades.

Since then, both in college and in graduate school, I've had more than my share of A's. But not one of them has ever meant as much to me as that final B+ awarded by Miss Leavitt for third-year Latin.—*Carol Zendman Howell*

A BULLEY PULPIT

Twenty or so nervous freshmen crowded into Room 312 for Music Appreciation, our first college class. Furtively, we searched for familiar faces or else avoided eye contact altogether with the still-strangers around us. Bending our heads over our desks, we scrutinized the inscriptions carved in joy and agony by generations past.

A lonely scuff echoed in the stairwell. The hallway door squeaked open, then banged shut. The old man entered the room in a cloud of smoke. A half-cigarette, half-ash, dangled from his lip. He walked with a stoop, panting from his climb to this belfry of a classroom. He shuffled to the desk, dropped books and papers in a crash, sighed heavily, and eased himself into the chair.

"My name is Dr. Stanley Bulley," he said, fumbling though folders. He squinted through his bifocals, leaned back so he could read through the lenses, turned the roster right side up, and intoned the roll as if inviting the faithful into a holy place to worship.

"I am not going to teach you facts about music," he announced. "You can get those from a record jacket. Most of them you'll forget." He smiled and closed his eyes. "I will use music to teach you how to think. We are here to expand our horizons."

Eager students all, we dutifully scribbled "expand horizons" in brand-new notebooks emblazoned with the college seal.

"Have we any music majors in the class?" he asked. I and maybe three others warily raised our hands.

"I will hold you to a higher standard than others in this class," he said matter-of-factly. "Remember that." Maybe I can drop this class, I thought, panicking. I'll find another section, another professor.

I stayed put.

Dr. Bulley's lectures were unnervingly complex, as he wove musical concepts from the threads of many disparate disciplines. This polymathic approach did not lend itself to traditional note-taking, the kind that allows a student to study and systematically review for the final exam. But, boy, did we learn about music. We learned to hear it and to appreciate the world from which it sprang.

When his digressions took on a life of their own, we chanted choruses of "Will this be on the test?" Sometimes he'd chuckle and tell us not to worry. Other times, he'd chide us for focusing on grades rather than on true understanding. "Put down your pens and listen," he'd scold as we busily transcribed his words into our notebooks.

But the kind of listening he was asking for required work. It lacked the usual formulas, a discernible starting place, a straight path, a destination. Dr. Bulley was asking us to trust that wisdom would reveal itself. He convinced us that wisdom retreats when faced with smugness, that it hides in plain sight, waiting to be invited into our lives. But he also warned that wisdom requires time to determine whether each of our souls will be a good home.

"You have come here to begin your education," he would tell us again and again, "not complete it. You'll find out how much you don't know. Then you'll expand your horizons."

As I struggled to trust Dr. Bulley, I discovered in music a fresh way of looking at the world—one that has proved indispensable to me throughout my life. I realized that I could figure things out without facts, that I could think through patterns and recognize them without data distracting me. As I developed patience, wisdom began to reveal itself through the haze of mere information. And, step by fitful step, Dr. Bulley applauded my efforts and encouraged the next step.

Dr. Bulley retired at the end of that semester. In the enormous chunk of time between my freshmen and senior years—it felt like a generation—I very nearly forgot about him. But just before graduation, as I packed away the accumulated detritus of four years, I came across my notes from that long-ago music appreciation class. On a whim, I found his number in the phone book and called to say thank you.

My phone call surprised him. Then he surprised me—by showing up at my graduation ceremony.

Decades later, I still regularly tap the wisdom Dr. Bulley unlocked. Whenever I encounter a new or puzzling problem, I say to myself, "Put down your pen and listen!" And most of the time, I like to think, I do just that.—*Carol P. Bartold*

MAKING A FINE MESS OF IT

He had a red birthmark on his cheek bigger than the one on Gorbachev's head. He was from Mississippi and smiled a lot and said we were going to be reading some "im-POH-tant LIT-er-a-too-er." Not "litercher" like I said but a genuine five-syllable aristocratic Southern word. I wish I could say I was entranced, but mostly I was scared.

He was the son of a preacher man, he said, a Baptist minister, and he had never been North before, but he was happy to meet us. His name was John McCully.

I was transferred out of his section the next week, into an Honors section, based on an embarrassingly naive essay on the assigned topic of race in America from someone who had never actually spoken to a black person. The next year, though still a pre-med student, I took his medieval literature course. God knows why. He remembered me and relished my shock. I had expected to be safely anonymous at this midwestern mega-university, after the close emotional confines of the small farming community I came from.

Notoriously disorganized, John would walk into each class with a stack of books too high to carry safely. They would tumble out of his arms, fall open, and scatter the torn bits of yellow paper that served as bookmarks. He'd scramble to gather them up, stop to apologize, then scramble some more, smile, then tell us what he would have read to us if he could find the page.

He also knew that he had something important to say. Somewhere in this mess of books was a great richness, and it was this messy teacher who had read them. As for myself, I could follow John's reading of them, but I never knew what I was supposed to do about it all, what to write or what to say. I would go sit on the bench outside his office, where I could read without being disturbed and without feeling that I was disturbing someone else. John might be in class and not due in the office for an hour, but I had that comforting bench by his door.

Inside the office was even better. There were books everywhere, and they all had bits of paper hanging out of them. He would grab an envelope out of the trash to write down an idea, in large, loopy handwriting that I tried to read upside down. He had an office-mate with whom he argued all the time. I came into the office on any pretense. I could hardly articulate a question, but they didn't seem to mind. They would go on arguing some point I only half understood, and I would listen to this strange new talk. I was not a part of it. I couldn't speak their language. I could barely write in imitation of it. But they let me listen in. This was my undergraduate education, and in some ways it was more powerful training than the Ph.D. ever could be.

I wish I could tell you that I did well in John McCully's medieval literature class, but I got an incomplete. It would turn into an F the next term, if I didn't write the papers. There was much to distract me: it was the Tet offensive. Bombs were dropping on the ancient city of Hue. I would be drafted in three more years. But that's not why I didn't complete the class.

I couldn't write the last paper because I still knew too little. John gave me a grade anyway, in defiance of my stubbornness and anxiety. It was an A or an A-, and totally undeserved.

He was like a father to me in the sense that I wanted to grow up to be like him. And he treated me with compassion, rather than according to my just deserts. I'm still trying to reach the level of devotion he showed to me, a debt I can only repay by passing the gift on to some other raw-boned, inarticulate kid who sits in my office not knowing what to say.—*James Persoon*

A NARROW ESCAPE FROM BOREDOM

I'm not really sure how I chose accounting as a major. A couple of my friends were accountants at one of the Big Six firms, and they were always talking about big corporate clients and working with millions of dollars. I probably thought, "Sounds great. I could make a lot of money." So when I enrolled in college, I signed up for accounting.

The only problem was that I was bored out of my skull. In class, I'd try to pay attention, but inevitably my mind would wander, and I'd start playing games on my computer or talking to friends. Accounting, I discovered, was the same thing day after day: follow a set of rules, do this, do that, then count up the numbers. The thought of doing this for the rest of my life was demoralizing, to put it mildly.

As part of my requirements, I had to take a marketing class. On the first day, a professor wearing a jaunty bow tie and a matching sweater-vest rolled into the classroom in a wheelchair. A guy sitting next to me whispered, "I wonder if he's going to be a really hard teacher." I asked him what he meant. The guy said, "He may have a grudge because he's disabled. He may be angry at the world." I didn't answer, but I thought it was a pretty bizarre thing to say.

Just how bizarre became apparent the moment Dr. Gordon DiPaolo opened his mouth. Unlike any teacher I'd ever known, he spoke to us as fellow human beings, not as students. He always said, "The only difference between us is that I've taken more credits than you have; that's why I'm on this side of the desk." There was none of the usual "I'm the professor, you're the peon—this is the way it's going to be, like it or lump it." He told us he wasn't concerned with grades, and we shouldn't be either. What mattered was where we'd go, what we'd do.

He made marketing so interesting that, whenever the bell rang, I'd say to myself, "Wait a minute, class just started." Sometimes he'd present us with a situation, and throw it out to the class for suggestions. "The Tide Corporation is looking to promote their new laundry detergent," he might say. "These are the conditions; these are the demographics. What would you recommend?" I'd never been much for class participation, but now I became one of the most vocal people in the room. For the first time in months, I actually felt challenged.

Professor DiPaolo was a big believer in collaboration. He'd divide us up into smaller groups, then say, "Here's a project: work on it together and come up with an answer." He told us he was training us for the real world, where we'd have to come together with all kinds of people from different backgrounds, whether we liked them or not, and work as a group to get something done. He was very concerned about our lives after college. He'd invite guest lecturers to class to tell us about "the real world," and he was constantly bringing in newspaper and magazine articles about careers, hiring practices, the job market.

He also cultivated an attitude of professionalism in all of us. On the first day, he told us, "Be on time for class. There's no excuse for lateness." Everyone said, "Well, what if my car won't start?" And he said, "Listen, when you get a job and you have to be there at eight, you can't tell your boss, 'Oh, my car wouldn't start.' For now, this is your job—to be in class from eight to ten."

And he never came in late, not once. One Monday morning—there had been a big snow storm the night before—everyone thought school would be canceled. Out of a class of fifty, maybe seven showed up that day, including me, because I lived nearby. And Professor DiPaolo was there early. I remember thinking, if this man who is partially paralyzed and in a wheelchair can get up at five in the morning to teach an eight o'clock class, then the least I can do is be there on time. (The funny thing is, I never viewed him as having a disability, and to this day I still don't know how he wound up in a wheelchair.)

By then, of course, I wanted to switch my major to marketing, but I was afraid there might not be any money in it. So I went to Professor DiPaolo, chairman of the marketing department, for advice. "I think you'd do better in marketing," he said. "You've put together some great projects, and you have some very clever ideas." He also assured me that there was money to be made.

That was all I needed to hear. I changed majors and excelled in marketing, even earning a scholarship from the college. Before graduating, I took four more courses with Professor DiPaolo. I became such a fixture in his classroom and got so fast at completing his tests, that the running joke was that after ten minutes of each test he would ask "Isaac, are you done yet?" And I'd say, "Yep, I'm done."

I'd stop to chat with him after class almost every day, and gradually we developed a friendship that is still very much a part of my life. When I got married in the summer of 1998, he came to the wedding, and last semester, he invited me to speak to his students about the public-relations field, in which I now work as an account executive. After I filled them in on public relations, I gave them some of the same speech I had heard just two years earlier in Professor DiPaolo's class—about preparing yourself, about getting out in the real world, about paying attention to what the professor was saying, because it was all true.

Then I recalled something else Professor DiPaolo would always tell us, class after class. "You're going to look back after you get out of college," he'd say, "and think, 'I wish I were there again.' " I never really believed it; like most college students, I was impatient to get started. But I when I spoke to his class, I found myself saying, "Let me tell you, I wish I were still in college." I love my work (a fact for which I have only Professor DiPaolo to thank), but, given the opportunity, I'd be back in his classroom in a heartbeat.—*Isaac Farbowitz*

SAINT NICK'S BAG OF TOYS

After ten years of teachers who said, "Don't get smart with me," we stumbled, underslept and overeager, into the class of one who actually wanted us to get smart with him. Many of us did not know what to do.

Nick's masterful instruction kept us all guessing, excited, surprised enough to learn in ways we'd never encountered before. The hard-core preps, the boys in stiff-pressed khakis and the scrubbed and skirted girls would panic, their GPAs teetering on unpredictability. They cried out for comprehensible multiple-choice, right-wrong, true-false cookie-cutter evaluations.

"Will this be on the test?"

"Does spelling count?"

"Do we have to memorize this?"

Nick was all too capable of hearing the underlying questions: "What do you want us to think? What should we learn? How will we know we are smart if you don't tell us how to get good grades?"

He would warn us of a test well in advance, building the tension for a week and a half. He'd hand us a poem, saying, "This could show up on the test," and then watch us read intently, trying to guess what questions he might put to us. The really "good" students, those accustomed to A's, pestered him for hints. Nick would threaten to subtract a grade for every such question, then watch their letter-dependent adolescent eyes widen in alarm. The next day, he'd hand us a story and steer us from discussion of the mysterious test to talk of the text we'd just read. When the day of the exam arrived at last, he said, "Take one and pass the rest down," just as every teacher always had. But what we took and what we passed along was a blank sheet of paper. As we looked to him for further instruction, he said simply, "You have thirty minutes."

Sad-smiled Nick had no interest in seeing us get good grades, and even less in telling us what to learn and what to think. He wanted only to spark the fire of learning and let it rage. He wanted us to distrust the grades and follow our intellects instead. With his cryptic messages on the blackboard—"Think" or "Question, don't ask"—he challenged us to challenge him. Where other teachers taught material, Nick showed us how to learn. Where other teachers instilled facts, Nick taught us to seek truth.

Like his namesake, Nick gave us gifts. Extravagant gifts. He eliminated the past experiences of traditional, staid teachers, and the future concerns of college admissions and progress reports and gave us the pure present, the ability to focus on what was happening now. He gave us the tools we needed to think for ourselves and showed us how to use those tools as toys—to play freely with thought, to read without pressure, to reason for pleasure, to rhyme without reverence. He inspired us to strive for Ginsbergian angel-headedness.

That inspiration alone was worth the price of admission.—*Dylan Brody*

CHAPTER SEVEN

Let There Be Light

If the "aha" moment is an epiphany, a revelation of blinding force, then its counterpart is a gradual dawning of recognition. The teachers who effect such enlightenment may awe us with their erudition, humble us with the sheer force of their personalities, or startle us with news of the universe outside our classroom. They are the ones who connect the dots, who make us see that what we're learning from them is part of a larger picture that, dot by tiny dot, is taking shape before our eyes. Clearly, it's no accident that, whenever people start talking about teachers who made a difference in their lives, such phrases as "a whole new world opened up to me" get repeated again and again. No matter what the method, these teachers permanently alter our vision, allowing us to enter a place we previously never knew existed.

These teachers help us grow up by enticing us to lose our innocence—not in a corrupt or cynical way, but by offering the fruit of the tree of knowledge. And once we take that first bite, as anyone who's been there can attest, there is no turning back.

TOOLS FOR LIVING

"Gonna go kill Bambi this weekend, Mr. Worman?" I teased as I gathered tools for the midterm in home maintenance. Earlier in the semester, while our class cleaned grease traps in the cafeteria sinks, our shop teacher had confessed his fondness for antique muskets.

Mr. Worman shook his head. "The musket's just an excuse to stomp around in the woods," he said. "I only aim at paper targets. I lost my taste for death in the war."

"The war?" I asked. "You mean World War II?"

"World War II," he said, nodding slightly. He glanced at his watch. "You've got fifty-five minutes to finish."

It was 1978, and there were six of us in all: eleventh-grade girls with an aversion to baking peanut-butter cookies and stitching A-line skirts, huddled around the blueprints for a small-scale grain silo. In the tiny Indiana farming community where we lived, this was the first year that girls at our high school were allowed to take shop as an alternative to home economics.

Mr. Worman leaned against a worktable and watched us from behind gold wire-rimmed glasses. I laid out wrenches, screwdrivers, and a power drill while my cohorts slid long pieces of curved corrugated aluminum out of heavy cardboard packaging.

Five months earlier, the shop had been a no-woman's land. Now, at midterm, I owned the place. I'd rewired a couple of old lamps, fixed a faulty wall socket, and replaced the washers in the school's bathroom faucets. At this point, I felt as confident with an array of tools as my father looked when he used them at home.

The six of us got down to business. I braced myself against two pieces of aluminum while another girl bolted them together. Late fall sunshine illuminated dust as it settled on Mr. Worman's nickel-gray hair. Mr. Worman was just a couple of years older than my father. It was one of the great disappointments of my dad's life that the war was ending just as he was graduating high school. Like most young men of his era, he had been champing at the bit to fight Hitler. Even now, Dad's favorite Christmas gifts were books about "The War."

While we pushed and sweated to align the silo's roof, I hummed "As Time Goes By."

"How do you know that song?" Mr. Worman asked.

"*Casablanca* is one of my favorite movies."

The roof finally cooperated. As we pushed the eight-foot-tall structure upright we slapped palms. Mr. Worman graded us on the spot: A+ for teamwork, B+ for the slightly skewed assembly.

I told the others to go to lunch while I put the tools away. When I finished, I asked, "Do you know the words to 'As Time Goes By'?"

Mr. Worman half-sang them as I sat cross-legged on a worktable and penciled them into a notebook filled with wiring diagrams.

"My favorite line from *Casablanca* was Humphrey Bogart's, when he's talking about Paris," I said. "He said, 'I remember every detail: The Germans wore gray, you wore blue.' "

"I was in Europe at the end of the war," he said. "Berlin."

"What was it like?"

As Mr. Worman talked, I imagined my father, heroic in hues of cinema silver, saving orphaned babies amid the city's skeletal remains.

"So it was a lot like The Big Lift in the movie?" I asked.

"That was actual footage," he said. He paused and stared off toward the narrow windows in the garage-style doors at the shop's far end. He described the city quiet and dark beneath a cap of starred sky, broken only by an occasional yellow glow at street level.

"People gathered around trash fires in the evenings," he said. "They sat on the shattered walls of their old apartment buildings."

Mr. Worman then described a crisp fall morning and the single heart-numbing thump of a mine or a mortar exploding at the edge of a bustling platz. A green-trimmed wooden streetcar, suddenly rose in orange flames. Rushing to help the passengers, he pulled out a woman, then a man. He reached in again and grasped a flailing forearm. He peered into a woman's wide-open face, her lips bright with fresh red lipstick, her eyes a pale and panicked blue. She fell away from him, into the flames.

"Her skin came off in my hands," Mr. Worman said, "like the peel on a scalded tomato." Her arm waved once from the heart of the flames. Then he looked down, smelling the stench and feeling the odd sensation of the woman's skin resting black and red in his palms.

Something moved behind Mr. Worman's blue-gray eyes. His soul pulled away, retreating for a moment to avoid contact with all that he had witnessed. "The Germans," he told me, looking into his hands, "were never faceless or invincible. They were as vulnerable as any of us is capable of being, and as terrible."

I left Mr. Worman's class that day with new tools for interpreting my world. The colors of war, it turned out, were nothing like the romantic shades of silver I had imagined, nothing like the comforting contrasts of black and white on celluloid.—*Sally Weigold Charette*

READING, WRITING, AND MRS. ROUSE

I was born into an impoverished tenant farming family in Orient, New York, where we lived in a large, drafty old farmhouse. My mother cooked on an old cast-iron stove in the kitchen, and the family would gather around it to keep warm. We possessed a grand total of maybe a dozen books, but I was fascinated with all of them. Once I learned to read, I pored over those precious volumes, reading them again and again, as if for some secret message.

Leila Rouse, who taught in the four-room schoolhouse I attended in the 1950s, opened a whole new world to me. Every day she read to us one chapter from Laura Ingalls Wilder's Little House series. Because Mrs. Rouse was my teacher for second, third, and fourth grades, I eventually heard them all more than once, but I never tired of them. That the author had actually once been the little girl in the stories thrilled and inspired me. Still, it never occurred to me that I, too, could write. When I spoke of books in my family, I was told that writers were crazy people who died in gutters.

During one summer vacation, I ached to hear those stories, but we lived too far from the nearest library to borrow them. And certainly we could not afford to buy them. Desperate, I wrote down all that I remembered of Wilder's tales. When I later told Mrs. Rouse, she said I could write my own stories. And that's just what I did, though for many years I hid what I wrote. It was a secret meant only for my soul.

People tell me I would have become a writer in any case. But I like to think it happened because a wonderful teacher took the time to read to her students, and in doing so, helped one little girl escape the despair of poverty on the wings of imagination.—*Diane Crawford*

COMFORT ZONE

In 1969, when I was five, kindergarten wasn't mandatory in Louisiana, so my parents didn't send me. It was a turbulent year in the town where we lived, a southern suburb of Baton Rouge. Systemwide desegregation (achieved by cross-town busing) of the area's public schools had recently been mandated, and there was picketing, rioting, and even a shooting near the public school my older brother attended.

I can still hear the urgency and apprehension in my parents' voices as they discussed the violence in hushed whispers, giving vent to their worst fears for my brother's safety. Of course, at five, I didn't fully grasp what was going on, but I understood enough to conclude that school was a scary, negative place that I wanted to avoid at all costs.

By the time I was six, though, I couldn't stay out of school any longer, so my parents enrolled me in first grade at East Ascension Academy, a newly formed private school in the area. My teacher was Mrs. Hazel Gregoire, who had recently retired from the public-school system after some thirty years of teaching and had now been pressed back into service by the directors of East Ascension.

There was nothing especially remarkable about Mrs. Gregoire—she was an ordinary-looking woman in her late fifties with beauty-shop hair and silver cat's-eye glasses dangling from chains on each side of her face—nor do I recall any deathless words of wisdom issuing from her lips. What I do remember are plenty of hugs (something kids today largely do without because teachers are so afraid of being misinterpreted), encouragement, and good old-fashioned structure. With her kind, gentle, and nurturing nature, Mrs. Gregoire utterly transformed my impression of school. Instead of the chaotic, threatening battle zone I'd pictured, I discovered a warm, welcoming haven.

The following year, the picketing and furor over busing subsided, so my brother and I switched back to our neighborhood public school. But I stayed in touch with Mrs. Gregoire, exchanging annual Christmas cards until well after I went off to college. When I graduated from high school, she wrote me a long, emotional letter about what it meant to watch a student evolve and grow over a twelve-year period. That letter is still among my most cherished possessions.

Her lasting influence on me is akin to that received by a child who gets read to constantly during infancy and toddlerhood and comes to associate books with the soothing memory of cuddling with a loved one. I'll be forever grateful to Mrs. Gregoire for showing me that school could be a comfortable place led by caring people. Because of her, my associations are all happy ones.—*Kelly King Alexander*

A WHOLE NEW WORLD

In eleventh grade, we were able to choose some of our own classes for the first time. Instead of a traditional history course, I took a philosophy class, called—astonishingly, even in those prepolitically correct times—"Men and Ideas." The teacher, Geoffrey Morrison, was new to my high school, and not particularly popular. He was too strict: on the first day, he informed the class that he expected the same level of work from us as he did from the college students he taught.

Mr. Morrison soon had us reading some pretty tough texts—Kant, Descartes, Plato—and talking about capital-letter concepts like Truth and Justice. After years of memorizing facts and dates, I was thrilled to be thinking about the big picture. The fact that my family wasn't particularly religious made ideas like Plato's distinction between the "real" and the "true" even more compelling.

But it was when we turned to "Symposium," Plato's treatise on love, that a whole new world seemed to open up for me. If you weren't concentrating really hard, the whole thing could go in one eye and out the other. But Mr. Morrison made sure that didn't happen—he actually diagrammed the "plot" for us on the blackboard! Plato thought that each of our souls was missing its other half and that when you fell in Love (capital L) with the right person, both of your souls flew up to the heavens and joined as one. I'd never even heard the phrase "my better half," and I was fascinated. (It sounds impossibly sappy when you describe it, but it was very academic at the same time.) I was extremely receptive to romantic notions, of course—what sixteen-year-old girl isn't?—but it was the realization that someone had thought and written these ideas thousands of years ago that truly amazed me.

I don't think anyone else in the class really got it, and Mr. Morrison knew that I did. It was exciting for him to see me get excited about these ancient texts to which he'd devoted his life (he'd recently received his doctorate). I worked hard in his class, partly because I loved the material, but also because I realized that I was making him proud. He was a rather introverted person, and he probably lost himself in his books. The fact that I appreciated the same things he did created a bond between us. In his class, I learned to think analytically—to look beyond the details, to home in on what the real issues are, and to make connections not always evident to other people. I felt more like a college student than the naive eleventh-grader I was.

When I actually got to college, though, I was frustrated for the first two years, partly because he had spoiled me. The Yale faculty didn't inspire me the way Mr. Morrison had, and I could find no subject that interested me enough to major in. I felt like a small fish in a big pond, surrounded by brilliant people whose own teachers had written recommendations just as glowing as the one Mr. Morrison wrote for me.

I couldn't figure out where my place was until I found the American Studies department. I liked the way its course offerings examined cultural history from a whole range of perspectives—literature, history, art, lifestyles—and tried to reconcile them. Suddenly, everything clicked, and now I understand why: The department took the same big-picture approach that had so captivated me back in Mr. Morrison's philosophy class.—*Diane Debrovner*

GREETINGS, SIR!

Dear Mr. Vandervliet,

Hello, sir! I hope this letter reaches you in good health. I'm so happy that I was able to compete against you on *Jeopardy*! I spoke to Alex Trebek after the show, and he said he'd never before seen a man of such knowledge in action. I am still amazed at your ability to recall facts almost automatically. It is almost as though your mother read the encyclopedia to you in the womb. Is that the secret? Does osmosis work?

After the show I overheard Alex say, "I never thought a person could be on the show for five days and only miss two questions!" I do, however, regret being on the receiving end of your sheer domination. You may remember that I was the one you beat out $52,000 to $2,100. I don't think the NASA scientist we competed against won *any* money.

I truly believe there is no feat of learning that is beyond you. I clearly recall my days in your U.S. history class, where your precise and meticulous way of teaching made students want to learn.

You were intimidating to some, loved by most, respected by all. I can see how some people could be intimidated by a teacher who maintained a perfectly buzzed haircut, wore thick glasses, never went out of the house without a shirt and tie, and could organize a list of U.S. presidents according to their height.

Your passion for education rubbed off on your pupils, and it is reflected by how well they have done in the classroom of life. You are the most organized and structured person I've ever met. I remember joking with my fellow students about what your house must look like. I always imagined a place that had a coatrack as you entered and not a speck of dust or clutter anywhere.

Your relentless pursuit of perfection in all you endeavor is a noble trait, and I am proud to say I was taught by a near-legendary educator. I hope that life is treating you well—why wouldn't it, after you won all that money?—and I am looking forward to our sitting down and conversing on a more adult level sometime soon. Perhaps over a game of Trivial Pursuit?—*Josh Fralick*

BLACKBIRDS AND BLUE-BOOKS

I hated school from the moment I hit kindergarten. My dad worked for the federal government, and he was transferred several times. I started kindergarten in Maryland, finished it in Kentucky. Started first grade in Kentucky, finished in South Carolina. Started second grade in one South Carolina school, finished it at another.

On the first day of third grade, they divided the students into three groups and pinned little paper birds to our shirts to signify which group we belonged to. There were the bluebirds, the kids who excelled in reading and math; the redbirds, who were average students; and the blackbirds, who were the slow learners—in today's jargon, the "academically challenged." I was a blackbird at age eight.

In fourth grade, it got worse: I was sent to special ed. But almost at once, I decided that special ed wasn't so bad: we read for an hour Monday through Thursday and got ghost stories on Friday.

The next year, at yet another school, I was placed in a regular class. But I quickly decided that the special-ed classes were the place to be: they had "talking machines" that ran with magnetized picture cards that spoke the word of the object in the picture. As intriguing as this was to a ten-year-old boy, the real attraction was the candy that was given out on Fridays. If you were unfortunate enough to be placed in a regular class, you got nothing—on Friday or any other day.

By fifth grade, I was at the top of my game. I not only got myself reassigned to special ed, but I also convinced the PE teacher to let me help build the new playground. That kept me out of all classes after lunch for four or five weeks. Even punishment, I learned, could work in my favor. The penalty for running in the hall was two days of weed pulling—during regular class time. So I ran like hell and was duly sentenced.

I was never a trouble-maker or rude to teachers, but I skipped a lot of classes and goofed off in the ones I showed up for. One of my high-school tricks was to ask a lot of questions to get the teacher talking about something other than the subject at hand; it was kind of like running out the clock when you're playing basketball. This technique worked very nicely. Until I met Terry Dozier.

Tenth-grade world history was taught by this petite, pretty, Asian-featured woman with long black hair. I tried my usual bag of tricks—stall, question, debate, anything to avoid discussing history. Nothing worked. After a few days, Miss Dozier curtailed my comments to two minutes, unless she had asked the question. Unfortunately for me, her questions required more brain activity than verbal virtuosity.

On the first day, Miss Dozier explained that her tests would not be the usual multiple choice but essays written in college blue-books. Spelling, grammar, and punctuation would count as part of the grade. Until then, I'd never taken a test that required an answer of more than a sentence or two. So it was no surprise when my first tests came back with F's. I could use words, but spelling them was another matter. My terrible spelling had given me a phobia about writing.

By this point in my academic career, I was maintaining a C average without much effort—in all but Miss Dozier's class, that is. But, having come from a blackbird background, I figured that was the best I could do. Then, one Saturday, I came home from an afternoon of fishing and heard voices in the living room. I peeked around the corner, and there was Miss Dozier sitting on the couch. I had no idea why she was there, but I knew it couldn't be good.

After she left, my mother lit into me. Miss Dozier had told her that I had potential but needed to actually do some work. She suggested that my mother buy me a small dictionary to carry around to help me spell. A few weeks later, in my Christmas stocking, I found a small Webster's pocket dictionary. Some Christmas present. But I did take it to school and use it. In the past, even when I knew the right word, I couldn't spell it. So rather than attempt and fail, I would substitute a simpler word that I was sure of. Now, I could look the word up in my dictionary.

What stumped me most about written tests, besides spelling, was planning. Before you started writing, you had to read the question top to bottom and think about what you were going to write. I'm somewhat impulsive to begin with, so I would start off in one direction and then switch in the middle. I'd end up with a disjointed mess.

I never learned to like those tests, but, with practice, I got a lot better at taking them. And our world history class was one of the few I didn't cut. I think I ended up with a B, whereas my other grades were all C's.

I never took another class from Miss Dozier, but I saw her from time to time during those last two years of high school. Her effect never really dawned on me until my first essay exam at the University of South Carolina when I was handed a little blue-book. As I sat there calmly planning my essay, I realized that Miss Dozier had known exactly what she was doing. Because of her, I had finally learned how to think. And because of her, I ended up doing well in college.

I finished my degree, then applied to USC's law school. I wasn't the pick of the litter, but I did pretty well. Not long after I began practicing at the firm where I am now a partner, I turned to my bookcase to look up something. There on the shelf were three thesauruses, a Black's law dictionary, a medical dictionary, a Webster's—and that little stocking-stuffer from tenth grade. I smiled, thinking of Miss Dozier.

The next time I was in Columbia for a meeting, I decided to look her up at my old school. When I saw her coming down the hall, I said, "I have something that belongs to you." I handed her that tattered little dictionary and told her about all the others I now owned.

"In that case," she said, "I'll keep this one. It means a lot to me."

Not as much as it means to me: that dictionary is a symbol of the first teacher I couldn't outsmart. No matter how hard I tried, I simply could not figure out a way not to do what she wanted. And clearly, her other students feel the same way. In 1985, Miss Dozier was honored first as South Carolina Teacher of the Year and then as National Teacher of the Year.

When I was a child, most of my teachers would have considered me expendable. But not Miss Dozier. I think about that a lot in my work as an attorney. One of my current cases involves a car that went off the interstate because the highway department refused to do anything about water draining across the road. My client was a passenger; his wife was driving. The guy is now totally disabled.

Twenty other cars had gone off the same place over a five-year period. "That's not so many," people say. "You're wasting our tax dollars, suing the state, making them do this frivolous work."

I guess it depends on how you define waste. All I know is, they repaved half a mile of that highway after I sued them.—*Mark Ball*

THE KIDS IN 2D

We felt sorry for the kids in 2D. Every morning around ten, we'd watch them trudge, single file, like unhappy ducklings, to the water fountain to take their fluoride pills. Even when they came over to our classroom for the Friday filmstrip, none of the 2Ders uttered a single word—not even to each other. We didn't know exactly what dreadfully boring lessons were being taught next door in Ms. Dorsey's classes, but we were certainly glad that we didn't have to find out.

In retrospect, I have a more realistic guess as to the goings-on in the other first-grade class: You raised your hand; you answered the question. You colored the school buses in your workbook a nice marigold yellow. Ms. Dorsey's prim navy suit and stiffly coiffed gray hair said it all: fun was fun, school was school, and never the twain shall meet. Certainly her classroom could not have been the prison I envisioned sixteen years ago; yet I know that had I been confined to learning how to add and subtract in that adjacent room, my whole philosophy of learning would be radically different.

I was one of the blessed bunch in 2G, with Ms. Pruitt as our teacher. Oh, we had to raise our hands, too—but we came to understand that it was out of respect for others, not a means of teaching obedience. Learning in our classroom was always an active, creative adventure. We could color our school buses whatever color we wanted—indeed, a yellow one probably wouldn't have earned a second glance.

To Ms. Pruitt, we were a group of individuals who could learn from each other's strengths and help improve each other's weaknesses. She not only preferred that we walk two-by-two down the halls, she also asked us to pick partners (different ones each time) so we'd have a team effort in sounding out the hard words in new reading assignments. In pairs, we'd spread out across the big, brightly lit classroom—under desks, in corners, near the coatracks—working together but independent of an authority figure, discovering the joy in accomplishing a task on our own.

In Ms. Pruitt's class, I developed a sense of confidence, a feeling that if I made the effort, I'd always figure it out eventually. Her teaching style also facilitated cooperation, open expression, and creativity—the qualities that I've since found to be essential to successful teamwork.

But I think that the most important lesson I learned from Ms. Pruitt—the one that overshadows all the rest—is that learning is fun and knowledge exhilarating.

I've never forgotten that, and if a boring class or two over the years has ever made me doubt, I always remind myself that a better teacher—one like Ms. Pruitt—could make the subject more interesting. I'm not sure I would have retained that faith if, back in first grade, I'd been one of the six-year-olds assigned to 2D.—*Nicole Micco*

WAKE-UP CALL

He spoke the way all justifiably egotistical college professors do—soft enough so that every student leaned forward, straining to hear what might be exam material, but at a quick enough pace so that someone was always raising a hand to request that he repeat his last sentence. Heaven forbid if we didn't copy it all into our notebooks!

"People pay me thousands of dollars to speak about what I know," he announced during my first day of Anthropology 210, "so you will not—I repeat, you will *not*—fall asleep during my class, nor will you daydream as I attempt to saturate your brains with something more useful than marijuana smoke." The words hit the center of my forehead like an arrow that just missed the apple above. He was looking right at me, talking right to me. I feared that, eventually, he would see right through me.

At the time, my attention span was marginally longer than that of a gnat. I was just beginning my second year at Emory University in Atlanta, a school burgeoning in popularity and competitiveness, both to get in and stay in. Most of my waking hours were spent agonizing about who I was and what I wanted to be in the "real life" that was rapidly encroaching. In between, I aimlessly roamed the campus and bar scene in search of true love. I had nightmares of being called upon in class as I gazed out the window, head tilted, eyes twinkling: "Um, Ms. Chudnofsky? Would you care to share with the class your disdain for academics and your hopeless crush on the lawn-mower boy outside?"

Fearing this kind of humiliation, I spent two long months sitting in the front row, scribbling fast and furiously every word that left Dr. Martin Kutner's lips, replicating his every chalkboard etching and overhead graph. Petrified of failing someone who didn't even know my first name, I never dared to speak, not even to ask a "smart" question. And then one night, at a sparsely attended theater production, I caught the intimidating know-it-all in the midst of his own magnificent dream, revealed to all from center stage.

I expected my entire anthropology class would show up for Dr. Kutner's wife's directorial debut—an autobiographical play that she had also written—if not to uncover some of the mystery behind the man, then at least to satisfy him with a raised hand the next morning when he asked if anybody had attended. But they apparently all had better things to do than apple-polish.

I, on the other hand, was looking forward to a night alone, away from the usual Amstel Lights, Marlboro Lights, and neon lights of my off-campus social life; the darkness of the tiny, saw-dusted theater was strangely comforting. So was the hoarse yet resonant voice speaking from behind the spreading stage curtains as it began to unfold the story of two young, starry-eyed lovers with a dream to go to Africa, to see and explore everything, and then to tell it all to others.

The words spoken by the actress who played Dr. Kutner's wife had the familiar tone of a once-spoiled child on the verge of adulthood. She, like her new husband, was lost, searching for answers to the thousands of questions she had about the world. I sat alone, my cheeks red-hot with exhilaration as this voice echoed my own fears and reassured me that even the most successful, the most scholarly, the most confident of men and women experience doubts and insecurities. Indeed, by his wife's accounting, Marty Kutner had a long list of them! It seemed that even brilliant scholars who make groundbreaking discoveries about the !Kung San people in Africa get tired, scared, and mad at their mothers for not sending enough care packages.

The highly successful Dr. Kutner had once been a dirt-poor idealist, and so had his wife. The two of them had been madly in love with science, the unknown, and each other. They got lonely. They made love. They made love and still got lonely. They were human. Just like me.

Moved and inspired by the play, I wrote in my journal through the night:"I am breathtaken. Overjoyed. Dr. Kutner is a real person! His heart trembles just like mine does . . ."

I was so happy to have "met" my teacher, even if it wasn't face to face. In class the next day I put my notebook aside, left the cap on my pen, and finally just listened, thinking hard about what Dr. Kutner said instead of copying it mindlessly onto blue-lined paper. I raised my hand, told him my name, and of course, asked a "stupid" question. He answered it without laughing or shaking his head in disappointment and then said that it was nice finally to meet me. It was as if I had awakened from a long sleep.

I don't know what came over me after class. I think I was still on a high from the play or from asking my first question, however insignificant. I ripped the pages out of my journal, and in a zombie-like trance, walked up to Dr. Kutner and handed them over.

"I wrote this last night . . . after the play," I murmured, looking down at my toenails and wishing I hadn't painted them blue.

He looked perplexed. "Thanks, I'll make sure my wife gets it."

"Well, actually, it's for both of you."

Then he smiled, still a bit confused, and placed the folded pages inside his coat pocket. As I walked away, I was overcome by the rush of anxiety any nineteen-year-old would feel after turning over her most private thoughts. But I felt oddly calm about sharing them; after all, Dr. Kutner and his wife had shared with me.

I still remember every part of the phone call I received later that evening, partly because no teacher had ever called my home, but mainly because of the warmth in his voice (to my chagrin, it seemed to come quite naturally) and the sincerity of his words.

"Thank you, Lisa," he said. "Margaret and I . . . well, we loved what you wrote. We loved that you shared it with us. She wants to speak with you, is that okay?"

I was shaking so much I had to hold the phone with both hands.

"Lisa." She said my name enthusiastically, but not as a question. "Honey, what you wrote was beautiful. You know you can't stop writing? You know that, right?"

I could barely speak. "You really think so?" I asked.

"You have nothing to worry about. You're on your way to wonderful things." She covered the mouthpiece of the phone as she coughed.

"So you liked my play?" she asked, chuckling softly, as if she was slightly embarrassed to ask. Her voice was hoarse, rather like that of the actress she had cast to play herself, but more so. It suddenly dawned on me that she was sick.

Dr. Kutner got back on the phone. He had been sitting next to her throughout our conversation. I could actually picture him curled up with her on the couch, his shiny wingtips turned over on the carpeted floor and her legs draped over his knees as they passed the phone.

She reminded me of my best-friend's mother, chatty but wise. He reminded me of no one I had ever encountered. I didn't want the conversation to end and for a while it seemed as if they didn't, either. Before they got off the phone with me, Margaret confirmed that she was ill; in fact, she was dying. She said it quickly, almost casually, and then changed the subject so that I couldn't respond. It's the only part of our conversation I don't remember clearly—that, and saying good-bye.

I haven't spoken with anyone since that night who made me feel as thankful to be right where I was.

The next day in class Dr. Kutner shook my hand the way a new pal will at the end of a pleasant evening. He had a friendly face when you looked straight at it, beneath the professor's beard and pensive brow. But I could also see a sadness in his eyes. Now I read the stiffness in his shoulders as the burden of his pain, not as the pomposity of a stuffy, arrogant professor.

I ended that semester with an insatiable curiosity about all kinds of new things—among them the miracle of life, human wisdom in every form, and the !Kung San people of Africa. I received an unspectacular grade in Anthropology 210, but I gained a mentor and the indelible memory of an extraordinary woman whose too-brief life was rich with love.—*Lisa Chudnofsky*

CHAPTER EIGHT

The Advocate

There are certain teachers who seem endowed almost from birth with an unshakable sense of justice, and when they go to bat for us, we are forever in their debt. These are the teachers who are willing to march into the principal's office and demand to know why a student has been treated unfairly, who champion the weak against the bullies, or who quietly and determinedly defy policies and cross boundaries to pluck a student from harm's way.

Even more often, these advocates battle the enemies within us—our fear of change or of failure; our lack of confidence in our own abilities; our downright dumbness about what's truly in our best interests. And occasionally they wage war against darker, more abstract forces—those of ignorance and small-mindedness. All of these teachers are profiles in courage, fearlessly rising up not merely to bite the hand that feeds them, but, occasionally, as one former student in this chapter puts it, to "swallow . . . it whole up to the shoulder." Then again, there are times when that's exactly what's needed to see that justice is done.

"HERE SHE IS . . . MISS IOWA"?

For most of my sixteen years, I had been the consummate conformist. So when, in 1975, I cut my waist-length hair into a crew cut and became a radical feminist vegetarian intellectual (or at least what passed for that in Marshalltown, Iowa), a large part of my motivation was to throw my high-school teachers for a loop. I was sick of being predictable, boring, and "good." I wanted to shock their socks off.

I ended up being shocked myself, by the reaction of my French teacher, Stanley Bechtel. Mind you, Mr. Bechtel was not one of the "cool" teachers who had beards and long hair, wore plaid bell-bottoms, and tried to be one of the gang. On the contrary, he had thinning hair, nerdy glasses, and a penchant for bolo ties. But there was a gleam in his eye that stemmed from a formidable intellect, a genuine interest in his students, and a slightly subversive streak. I may not remember how to conjugate the French subjunctive tense, but I have many fond memories of our class sitting under a tree outside and debating world politics.

Mr. Bechtel had always encouraged me to express myself (despite my painful shyness), but now he became my enthusiastic champion. He introduced me to an instructor of transcendental meditation, shared cutting-edge political jokes, debated the nuclear threat—in short, began treating me like a peer, not a pupil. I believe it was my first experience of adult friendship.

One day, after class, I confided my greatest fantasy to him: to enter a beauty pageant, find a way somehow to win it, and then go onstage to denounce the whole extravaganza as a sexist sham. Leaping on the idea, Mr. Bechtel urged me to grow my hair again ("buzz cuts don't 'cut it' at beauty pageants," he pointed out), hone a pageant-marketable talent (I had a decent voice; surely I could work up a passable rendition of "Feelings"), and practice answering questions in the wholesome, determinedly upbeat manner so beloved by beauty-pageant contestants everywhere (I actually entered the state speech contest to debate the merits of the ERA—and placed second).

How I loved spinning this scenario with Mr. Bechtel! I'm not sure if I would ever have summoned up the nerve actually to go through with it, but my attention got diverted in any case. That summer I was accepted, along with a few other supposedly highly ranked eleventh-graders from around the country, into the National Science Foundation Economics

Institute, for college credit. I was terrified to go, believing I had no true aptitude for the subject. But Mr. Bechtel knew better. He kept telling me what a great opportunity it was to expand my horizons. So instead of beauty-pageant regimens, I got a dose of graduate-level college economics—and a first taste of independence.

I will be forever grateful for Mr. Bechtel's faith in me. I conquered some of my greatest fears that summer—fear of math, of leaving home, of changing my safe, narrowly defined version of myself. If I could entertain the idea of winning a beauty pageant, then certainly I could imagine myself doing a punch-card computer regression analysis!

By the time I returned for senior year—a much more confident and extroverted person—my thoughts, naturally, were focused on college. My beauty-pageant fantasy got forgotten amid the frenzy of SAT scores and financial-aid applications. But I've never forgotten Mr. Bechtel and the heady rush of being treated as a true equal.—*Julie Bain*

IMPOSSIBLE DREAMER

At Clifford Scott High School in East Orange, New Jersey, in the 1960s, I was a straight-A student with lots of ambition and no money.

Whatsoever. I don't mean my family was financially strapped. I mean we were poor—dirt poor. A too-small rental apartment. No phone, no car, no television, no washing machine.

I wanted to go to college, of course, but I expected that if I got to go at all, it would be to a small local school where I would commute to class. Even then, I knew I'd really have to struggle to get the tuition together. Then, in my final year of high school, my father died suddenly of a heart attack. As a result, my mother, who was schizophrenic and deaf, went back into the mental institution where she'd spent the better part of my adolescence.

That left just me and my brother, who was a year younger, on our own. Since I was of legal age, the authorities let him stay with me so we could finish school together. (My aunt, in a different county, agreed to look in on us from time to time.) My father's insurance left us with barely enough to live on for a year, and my mother was unable to work. There went my dreams of college, up in smoke. I figured I'd have to go straight to work right after graduation.

But Cora Stein, my guidance counselor at CSHS, insisted that I apply to Ivy League schools. I couldn't even afford the application fees, so she offered to pay them for me. She told me that if a top school accepted me, I'd have a good chance of getting scholarship money.

So, emboldened by her faith in me, I went for it. And Barnard College not only accepted me, it gave me a full scholarship, including a stipend to purchase my textbooks. My brother and I were both seniors in high school together. When we graduated, he enlisted in the Army and ended up in Vietnam. He was shot but survived—an experience that haunts him still. And I went off to study pre-med at Barnard College in New York City. (I never became a doctor, but I found my way back to the health field by becoming an editor of health books.)

Looking back at the terrified, vulnerable, unworldly eighteen-year-old that I was then, I shudder to think what would have become of me without Cora Stein in my life. It is difficult to express how deeply indebted I am to her. By believing in me and steering me in the right direction—in other words, by taking her job seriously and doing it well—she put me on course to a good education. And with that, she made everything else possible.—*Alice Feinstein*

THE WORLD BEYOND THE WALLS

In the spring of my second year at the United States Naval Academy, it dawned on me that I no longer wanted to be there. Getting in had been a lifelong goal, but now it was 1969 and the world beyond the Academy's walls had become an exciting place full of turmoil, soul searching, and sexual abandon. Within its walls, there was almost no indication that we were even in college. I had only a dim sense of all that I was missing, but I knew I wanted out, the sooner the better.

Getting out, however, was no small undertaking. An aggressive draft and the enormous weight of family expectations kept many a disillusioned midshipman in uniform. In my case, the weight was heavy indeed: My father was a career naval officer, and all my life, and a good part of his, I had wanted only to go to the Naval Academy and follow in his professional footsteps. Had it not been for the encouragement of one impassioned young instructor, I might never have had the guts to leave and become something of my own choosing.

In those years, the Academy was little more than an overblown trade school. Discussion of Vietnam, which was Topic One on college campuses everywhere else, was at Annapolis limited to comparative study of weapons systems or the retelling of grotesque war stories that had filtered back to us from recently graduated colleagues. Perhaps most discouraging of all for me, a history major, was the fact that all of the liberal disciplines were squeezed into one small English, History, and Government Department, referred to in the none-too-subtle slang of the then all-male Brigade of Midshipmen as "Bull." Yet it was in that department that I found the only semblance of the life of the mind that I thought I had gone to college to pursue.

To be sure, it was terribly thin even in Bull. One important exception was a young political-science instructor just out of an Ivy-League graduate school. He was alone among the faculty in conveying even the slightest excitement about what he was doing. And in his excitement, I had a tiny, tantalizing glimpse of the college life I was missing—one of eager intellectual exchange and open questioning.

One day after class, I approached this teacher and confided my longing to leave the Academy. His first reaction was feigned indifference. But after I brought it up to him three more times, he finally looked me in the eye and said, "You're really serious about this, aren't you?" Ushering me into his office, he shut the door and spent the next two hours exhorting me to do everything I could to get out of the Academy. "What everyone else in college is getting," he said, "and you at Annapolis are not, is an education in learning how to learn. For whatever reason—because of the war, because of the bureaucracy, because of legions of old admirals in Washington who think that all that naval officers need to know is how to plot a course and steer a ship—you are not getting that here. But once you have learned how to learn, you can do anything, you can solve any problem, and you will always grow."

It was the first time in two years that I had encountered anyone in authority who cared at all about education in its grander sense and not merely as an aid to navigation or as a tool of warfare. With the inspiration of this teacher and his simple insight into all that I had missed in two years of higher education, I finally mustered the courage to jump ship.—*Peter Lemos*

BEAUTY IS AS BEAUTY DOES

Until I met my fourth-grade teacher, my mother was the most beautiful woman in the world, but Miss Kolos beat even her out. She was slender, with jet-black shoulder-length hair; she dressed in silk blouses and wool skirts; and she was as kind as she was pretty.

Miss Kolos did things differently from any teacher I had known in my brief academic career. All the others retreated at lunchtime to the secret sanctuary of the faculty dining room, desperate, it seemed for a respite, however brief, from their students. Miss Kolos didn't seem to want or need that break; she ate lunch with us, as if she really liked our company. She even taught us table manners. To this day, when I slowly push the spoon away from me through my soup, I think of Miss Kolos.

I loved everything about her. Her perfume, the charm bracelet that clanked as she leaned over my desk to correct my work, the fact that she was so proud of her Greek heritage and taught us to be proud of our own ethnic backgrounds. But it was not just her charm or her beauty or the fact that she liked us that made Miss Kolos so special.

The story I cherish most is about Billy, a student who came from an abusive home and whose father was a drunkard. Realize that in the mid-1960s, no one where we lived talked about such unsavory matters as divorce or welfare or alcoholism or abuse. But one day after lunch, Billy had his head down on his desk. He was sobbing. No one knew what to do. To our relief, Miss Kolos entered the classroom.

"Why are you crying, Billy?" she asked gently. "What's wrong?"

"I'm hungry," he said, tears streaking his unwashed face. "My stomach hurts real bad."

Then Miss Kolos did the most amazing thing I had ever in my life seen a teacher do. She took Billy's hand, brought him to the cafeteria, opened it up (as we later learned), and made him lunch. While he ate, she sat and talked with him for almost an hour.

As our classroom buzzed with curiosity, I sat at my desk thinking about Miss Kolos and Billy. Then I did something I had never done before in my young life. I got out of my seat without permission. I had no choice, because there was no one to ask permission of. I stood in the doorway and watched down the hall until I saw the two of them walking toward me, holding hands. Billy's face was clean and smiling.

The wrath of God—or at least that of our unforgiving principal—probably fell on Miss Kolos's head that day. For that day, she broke all the rules. I knew—I heard the secretaries talking.

That year, I'm sure I learned about Brazil, and Lincoln, and long division. I don't remember. What I did learn was the importance of compassion, of having principles (and the strength to uphold them), and of taking risks for others.—*Barbara A. Rouillard*

A GRAND EXPERIMENT

Autumn in Albany. My film crew and I were doing our best to maneuver through the hall in the Capitol building, which was stuffed with journalists, news crews, dignitaries, well-wishers, and relatives. Seated around a large central conference table were members of the New York State Board of Regents, the body charged with setting the state's educational policy.

John Taylor Gatto, a New York City English teacher who'd taught junior-high-school English for twenty-six years, was about to receive the state's highest honor: Teacher of the Year. He was also the subject of my documentary. A bear of a man, Gatto, dressed in one of those multipocketed khaki fishing jackets, sat at the head of the table, surrounded by somber looking officials. As chaos whirled about him, he busily annotated a jumble of papers.

My crew and I grabbed a spot that gave us a decent angle, set up our tripod, and stuffed a radio lav-mic wire down Gatto's shirt. The commissioner of Education entered: "Ladies and Gentlemen, it is my singular honor each year to present the state's highest . . ."

Cameras flashed, our 16mm rolled, my eyes began to roam the oil portraits on the walls.

Twenty-five years earlier, I had been a student in John Gatto's eighth-grade class on Manhattan's Upper West Side. Although no single seminal memory of that year pushed its way to the front of my brain, I could say without hesitation that Gatto was the finest teacher I'd ever had—and I'd had some extraordinary ones.

The commissioner brought his remarks to a close, and Gatto walked to the podium accompanied by polite applause. The Regents' faces were frozen in mindless grins.

John's speech began as all such speeches do: "Thank you for this special honor . . . for myself and my family . . ." His reading glasses nudged down his nose, giving his voice a slightly congested sound.

The year I was in his class, he tossed away the approved curriculum and laid out a course of study that was as rigorous as any I later had in college. We began by closely analyzing the newspaper. We learned to read for what was printed as well as for what wasn't, and to distinguish the editorial position of each of New York City's major papers. Next we tackled poetics, memorizing and reciting large chunks of Coleridge and Shakespeare. We wrote monthly book reports that were so well structured that, four year later, as a senior in honors English, I simply tore off the covers and handed the exact reports to my teacher, receiving A+'s. Gatto assigned *Moby Dick* to the class and guided us through a reading so deep that all of American literature and history was forever made accessible through the prism of Melville's opus. He then broke the class into teams, each of which was required to present a fully annotated research paper on a topic of its choice. My team tackled the Warsaw Ghetto uprising. Gatto launched a chess club and a film society. During class, we watched and learned how to critique such films as *Night and Fog*, *The Lonely Boy*, and Mumford's *The City*. We devoured the work. Gatto assumed we could handle the load, and we did.

"We have fashioned a disaster in our schools that can no longer be concealed, nor is it subject to a quick fix by tinkering . . ." Suddenly, the Regents' glazed expressions began to tighten.

"This catastrophe extends far beyond the urban slums, reaching deeply into the finest homes and private schools as well . . ." His voice began to pick up momentum.

I remembered that voice. As a fourteen-year-old, I was awed by its tremendous variety and energy. He would sometimes shout, pounding the desk with his fists to emphasize a notion. Or laugh with glee when one of us would make a particularly sharp point. Or whisper to draw our attention to a subtle idea. His face, ringed with prematurely gray curly hair, wore a devilish expression. He never lectured, but spoke to us as peers, assuming we were all on the same quest for knowledge. His approach to teaching in those days was simple: he taught what he wanted to learn himself. He was delighted, not embarrassed, to be able to learn from his students, and he acknowledged our perceptions with sincere compliments. Unlike most teachers, he saw us as individuals instead of some abstract theoretical equivalents of adolescence.

"Confining a child with strangers for almost every day of his natural youth, denying him any rudimentary privacy, confining him in a class structure . . . conditioning him to bell/buzzer response, at short intervals . . . all these things are bizarre perversions of life. No culture in human history except our own would mistake these procedures for education . . ." Now, the Regents were beginning to look a bit pale.

Year after year, I went back to visit Gatto, always finding a crowd of his former students waiting to chat with him. Even then, I could see that he was not particularly comfortable with his status as a cult hero. Some fundamental change was incubating in the man's soul.

"[These perverse practices] destroy the ability to think independently, to value quality, to concentrate, and even, I think, to love each other . . . . We have institutionalized the division of social classes in our school classes, and used the police power of the state to create a caste system, complete with millions and millions of untouchables."

At this point, the Regents began to look to one another, their faces registering pain. The commissioner shifted nervously in his seat.

Somewhere around his fifteenth year of teaching, Gatto radically modified his approach. He created and administered an experimental program called the Lab School. He began sending his students out of the classroom, out of the school building, on special projects. Classic teaching became a much smaller part of his curriculum. He stirred the mix of his classes, making sure that the most privileged children sat next to the poorest. He broke the institutionalized racism of classroom "tracking" and enlisted the kids themselves to serve as instructive examples of bias and entitlement.

I visited his classes often in those days. I was teaching part-time myself, and several times a week I'd take groups of his students to Central Park. We wrote, edited, and published books of their poetry.

"The crisis in the general community is begun and nurtured by the school structures we maintain—all the dependency pathologies: drugs, television, commercial entertainments, alcohol and more, grow directly from the dependency we force upon children from the first grade onwards; all the aimless quality of our culture is a mirror of the school-room where millions of children are confined, unable to fill their own hours, unable to initiate lines of meaning in their own existence."

His speech concluded, Gatto thanked everyone again and promised to do his best in the year ahead. The Regents sat stunned and silent as the room erupted in applause and Gatto was thronged by reporters. Never before had anyone accepted this honor with such devastating grace. Gatto had not only bitten the hand that fed him, he'd swallowed it whole up to the shoulder.

During the last several years of his career, Gatto deepened his experiment. In one of Harlem's most troubled schools, he taught the classes considered the most unmanageable. He developed a program where kids spent no more than one day a week in school. The core of their work included internships, independent study, community service, and field work. His students blossomed, winning essay contests, making speeches, and landing good jobs. By now, he had thoroughly rejected the role of guru, instead placing the onus of education squarely on the students' shoulders. He would serve as coach or mentor—as a resource but never again as the primary wellspring of knowledge and approval. The only lesson worth teaching, he felt, was to be self-teaching.

But Gatto had sinned. He had blown the whistle on some of schooling's dirtiest secrets. The New York State educational apparatus would not allow itself to be so embarrassed, nor made so vulnerable again. A much tighter screening process was instituted for Teacher of the Year. And Gatto was discredited. His ability to teach the way he wanted to was systematically restricted. Nine months after receiving his award, Gatto published his letter of resignation in *The Wall Street Journal*.

Since quitting, Gatto has written three books, traveled, and lectured at locales as varied as the Kesey-inspired "Hog Farm" in Kentucky to the NASA Space Center. The documentary I began as an exploration of one extraordinary teacher has grown in scope. Now it asks a larger question: what is the real purpose of school in America?

"I've come slowly to understand what it is really I teach: A curriculum of confusion, class position, arbitrary justice, vulgarity, rudeness, disrespect for privacy, indifference to quality, and utter dependency. I teach how to fit into a world I don't want to live in . . . . There isn't a right way to become educated; there are as many ways as fingerprints." (John Gatto, "I Quit, I Think" *The Wall Street Journal*, July 25, 1991)

In his quarter-century career, there was no single lesson Gatto set out to teach. Rather, he served as a mirror to the 3,000-plus students. His great strength was that he reflected us back to ourselves. He empowered each of us to find our own way. And he conspired with us as we plotted our escapes from the confines of a system designed, it seemed, to do anything but truly educate.—*Roland Legiardi-Laura*

"MR. CAP"

Fred Capozella was the chairman of my high school English department, a literate man with a degree from a prestigious local college. But to the half dozen or so of his students who used to hang around in his office before and after school, he was simply Mr. Cap—short, bald, with black-rimmed glasses that made him look like a lovable nerd. He was fun and funny, with an easy laugh. He was probably nearly twenty years older than we, but in his office he treated us as equals, listening intently as we offered our opinions on politics, movies, music, and the most recent episode of *Saturday Night Live*.

He laughed at our jokes and our off-key renditions of the satirical songs of Tom Lehrer, and seemed genuinely interested when we told him what new pieces we were working on in orchestra. But he never played favorites in the classroom: I still remember how awful I felt when I tried faking my way through a discussion of *Moby Dick*. It was obvious I hadn't read the book, and Mr. Cap wasn't going to let me get away with that just because he appreciated my sense of humor.

Indeed, Mr. Cap had an unerring sense of fairness—and in senior year, I was its grateful beneficiary. From as far back as I can remember, I'd wanted to be a writer. In eighth grade, I decided to become a newspaper reporter. My father, who had recently died, had gone to journalism school before becoming a rabbi, but my inspiration was John-Boy Walton, specifically the episode of The Waltons where he decides to become a journalist, because it will allow him to write and earn a living.

I began writing for the newspaper my freshman year. At a high-school journalism conference during my junior year, I won a writing award and was told I'd go to another conference the following year. But when the conference rolled around, the editors (all high-school students) decided to take a freshman whose brother had edited the paper the year before. The newspaper advisor said he couldn't change the editors' minds. I was crushed, but I sensed it was pointless to keep arguing.

I didn't plan to complain to anyone, but Mr. Cap could tell something was wrong. One afternoon, when I was the only student in his office, he asked me what was going on. I told him the whole story, and when I finished, he stood up. "Come with me," he said.

"Where?" I asked.

"To the assistant principal's office," he said. "You're going to tell him what you just told me."

"It won't make a difference," I said. "They said there's no room."

"Never mind that," he said. "Just come with me."

Mr. Cap stood by me while I talked to the assistant principal, who seemed equally disgusted about what had happened. "The students aren't supposed to be making those kinds of decisions," he said.

Within a day, the editors invited me to the conference. But I was told I'd have to take public transportation—the conference was fifty miles away—because there was no room in the advisor's car. Maybe it was unreasonable, but if I couldn't go with the rest of the staff, I didn't want to go at all. Taking the Greyhound bus alone and showing up only because the editors had been forced to invite me made me feel like the ugly stepsister. So I chose not to go.

Mr. Cap understood. But I still had another problem to deal with: whether to keep writing for the paper. Was wounded pride a good enough reason to resign? As difficult as it may seem from the vantage point of adulthood, whether or not to continue writing for the paper was the most difficult and painful decision I'd ever had to make. I remember leaning on Mr. Cap's desk, fighting (unsuccessfully) not to cry.

"I want to keep writing," I sobbed. "I want to be a journalist. And how am I going to explain on my college application that I don't write for the school paper?"

"It's okay," Mr. Cap said, passing the tissue box. "You've worked for the paper for more than three years. And after what's happened, I can understand why you'd want to quit. It won't hurt your chances."

He was right—I was accepted, early decision, into journalism school. Not long after I handed in my resignation from the paper, a friend and I started our high school's first literary magazine. Five years after I graduated from high school, it was still running—and I was working as a newspaper reporter. My only regret is that I have yet to appreciate *Moby Dick* the way Mr. Cap did.—*Debby Waldman*

DQ

In her knee-high boots and plaid minidress, my new geometry teacher rose like the *Birth of Venus* above the sea of standard Formica desks in my tenth-grade classroom. This was at Bogside, a regional high school in central Massachusetts populated mostly by the children of Polish immigrants (so nicknamed because its squat brick-and-cement presence sat in what was once a bog). Those immigrants were now largely unemployed and alcoholic, thanks to factory closings that had turned once-humming mills into silent, shut-eyed brick giants. Needless to say, these children were not keen about geometry.

In fact, most of these tenth-graders were not keen about much of anything: their parents drank, and so the kids drank and smoked dope, too—secretly from paper bags stashed in their lockers or openly during parties at The Rock, a place where, my first party there, I witnessed a classmate get stoned enough to try Tarzanning from one birch tree to another. (He was left partially paralyzed—though not too paralyzed to flip his Corvette one icy night the following year.)

The geometry teacher, who introduced herself as Judith DeCew but said "DQ" was okay by her, arrived during my first full year at Bogside. Like me, she was a foreigner: she spoke in what I later decided was a crisp boarding school vernacular amid the forgotten "R's" and lapsed grammar of central Massachusetts. She might as well have been from Mars. I suppose that was what drew me to her in the first place—that, and because she had the heart and head to convince me that surviving adolescence was not that different from surviving geometry.

I had arrived the semester before, unhappily transplanted by my father, a Navy man, and miserable from the start. The students at this school had been together since kindergarten, and my status as the new girl—and one who was exotic to boot, with my odd southern accent, passion for horses, goody two-shoes attitude toward academics, and relative wealth (given the fact that my father was steadily employed)—provoked everything from curiosity to envy. The boys, of course, were interested: Here was a Girl Type they'd never encountered before. And so the girls were infuriated. Three of them—big, square, and sturdy of limb and tooth—waited every day in the bathrooms, hoping for an opportunity to cuss me out, if not to blacken my eye. They followed me home after school, pitching rocks at my head. And once, as I waited for my mother to pick me up after school, the gang pulled me into the locker room, stripped off my clothes, and threw me into a scalding shower.

I couldn't tell my parents because the gang threatened to kill my younger brother if I uttered a word. So I came home every day after school, mute and shocked, to lock myself in my bedroom and do my homework.

This went on until, some months into my first year at Bogside, as an act of self-preservation I began "going out" with the older brother of this gang leader. This boy did a cartwheel in the snow when I agreed to be his girlfriend. He was my somnambulist partner in Spanish lab and a constant troublemaker. I was president of the Spanish Club and an A student. We were perfect together. After he beat up his sister, the gang leader, and her two buddies as well, peace reigned.

Until, that is, I tried to break up with him. That's when DQ saved my soul, if not my life. During the beginning of sophomore year, as I was learning to love the logic of proofs and the beauty of shapes, my Spanish teacher—a mild-mannered bespectacled man who still lived with his elderly mother—offered me the opportunity to travel as a "student ambassador." This honor stemmed from the fact that I was really his only student in a class of ninety-one sophomores (only five of whom would go on to four-year colleges) who had learned any Spanish at all. Excited, I chose Argentina out of all of the possible destinations, simply because it was the farthest away.

My boyfriend didn't want me to go, naturally, so I broke up with him. And then he cried. "I'd lie down in front of a truck for you!" he sobbed, just before he hurled a chair at me across the school cafeteria, hard enough to dent the lockers behind me when I ducked.

I told him I wouldn't go. How could I leave someone who loved and needed me so much?

And then, thank heaven, DQ intervened. She called me into the classroom one day, under the pretense of asking if I would be interested in competing in the regional math and science fair. I would not, I told her unhappily. I could not do one thing more than I was already doing.

DQ looked at me for a long time. I studied her, too: the long blonde streaks in her hair, the tan, slender arms that I had overheard another teacher mocking. ("Nobody should be that tan in winter," she had hissed to a colleague one day as I toiled away on the potter's wheel. "Who does she think she is, flaunting her trip to the Caribbean?")

"It won't always be like this, you know," DQ told me.

"What won't be?" I asked.

"Love. Life. Being." She spread her hands. "You will become someone else. You're a bright kid. You'll leave here, if not to travel right now, then later. And every experience you have will matter, so even if it's a terrible time at the moment, it still counts." She tipped her head, the long hair sliding over one shoulder. I couldn't take my eyes off that hair. "Do you have any idea what you want to do?" she asked.

"I want to go away," I whispered.

She smiled, the smile like a benediction. "Then do it."

And so I did. I went to Argentina, and then off to college. After graduation, I found a job as a copy editor for an academic journal at Harvard. That's where I ran into Judi DeCew again. She was working on her doctorate, not in mathematics but in philosophy. Just one conversation with her convinced me that I, too, could go to graduate school. What's more, I could do it in creative writing, the one passion that had stayed with me through all the good, the bad, and the indifferent times I'd weathered since being at Bogside. Her example showed me that I could follow my passion, even though I'd had every intention of pursuing a sensible career that would protect me from the world.

Still later, as a freelance writer researching a magazine article on feminism, I discovered that DQ had joined the faculty at Clark University, where I had earned my bachelor's degree. I felt no need to see or talk to her; it was thrilling just to glimpse her name in my alma mater's catalog. It confirmed that I was still connected to the one teacher who had helped me realize that life is not just a conveyor belt, where you get on at one end and wait until the ride is over, but a series of choices. She inspired me to take charge of my fate—and whether I made the wrong choice or the right one was beside the point. What mattered was the experience of making it, living it, and growing from it.

—*Holly Robinson*

CHAPTER NINE

Eccentricities and All

Tucked away in nearly everyone's book of memories is at least one teacher who is inevitably described as a real character—a bit screwy maybe; probably amusing; perhaps maddening; always unpredictable. These are the teachers we end up dishing about at class reunions—after the dinners and the speeches and the not-so-subtle discussions of the alumni fund, when everybody repairs to the local pub to talk about what really went on back in the good old days. We loved these teachers in spite of their eccentricities, and often because of them.

For better or worse, we tend to place educators on pedestals. Yet, ultimately, it is their quirks, be they charming idiosyncrasies or appalling flaws, that humanize teachers and enable them to work their particular educational alchemy on us. With their corny jokes, their oddball habits, their larger-than-life theatrics, these unforgettable personalities turn education into the highest form of entertainment.

AN UNLIKELY MUSE

Everyone was in love with Mrs. Demme, one of two fourth-grade teachers. She dressed in silky shirtwaists and wore her auburn hair in a French twist, like Inger Stevens in *The Farmer's Daughter*. In June, every third-grader prayed to be assigned to Mrs. Demme in September, instead of to Mrs. Stohl, who was short and dumpy and wore too-tight pastel suits. Her black hair was rock-hard with spray. Her eyes, squinty behind rhinestoned glasses, missed nothing.

During assembly, a sweet-voiced, sweet-tempered Mrs. Demme led us in song, accompanied by Mrs. Stohl on the piano, who, in flagrant violation of the NO FOOD IN THE AUDITORIUM rule, kept a sixteen-ounce cup of Coke beside her on the piano bench and Milky Ways hidden behind the sheet music. If too many chairs squeaked during announcements, or if someone bothered his neighbor while we sang "Look for the Silver Lining," she'd stomp on the damper pedal, raise both hands ominously high in the air, and crash down on the bass keys. (I later borrowed this technique for my composition "Thunder and Lightning" on the family piano. My parents failed to appreciate it.)

My prayers were ignored. In September I lined up in the schoolyard with the other unfortunates and followed Mrs. Stohl as she marched up the steps and down the hall, rapping a wooden pointer against the freshly painted wall. As we passed Mrs. Demme's room, even the notorious Henry Burton and Bobby Simon peeked in longingly.

Mrs. Stohl was rumored to go through hundreds of pointers every school year. Those rumors, we soon learned, were true. She never hit anyone, but she smashed the pointers against desks, blackboards, and walls. She kept several within easy reach, should some fool dare to whisper or pass notes or copy from his neighbor's paper. Every diagrammed sentence or subtraction problem was accompanied by the click-click of her pointer against the blackboard. While we labored over vocabulary words or the characteristics of metamorphic rock, Mrs. Stohl policed the aisles, looking for gum chewers or desk carvers or daydreamers or cheaters. We'd hear the creak of the floorboards under her high heels and hold our breath. At the inevitable CRACK! we'd jump six inches in our seats, involuntary screams escaping our lips.

The guilty culprits were usually Henry Burton or Bobby Simon or less often, Sally Shaffer, who looked like a rough draft of Pippi Longstocking. Still, no one was entirely safe.

But Mrs. Stohl's bite was all bark. By Christmas, Henry Burton and company were up to their old tricks. Mrs. Stohl continued to smash pointers and we continued to flinch, but more out of habit than fear. In the late afternoon, as we waited for the bell, Mrs. Stohl sometimes read poetry to us. I remember Walt Whitman, Emily Dickinson, and Mrs. Stohl's favorite, Joyce Kilmer. (Years later, as a college freshman, I was shocked to hear Kilmer's famous "Trees" dismissed as bad poetry.)

Then for Flag Day, to deep groans, Mrs. Stohl assigned us to write our own poems. I sat down dutifully that evening and discovered—not patriotism, but words. I was a goner.

Mrs. Stohl praised my poem, "The Flag," and read it to the class. She asked me to write some more. And so, in the evenings while my sisters and brother pounded the piano or watched TV, I labored alone at the kitchen table in the dim yellow light. I was word-drunk, reeling with adjectives, running wild with adverbs. I wrote about a black stallion and about the sea, which at that point I'd barely seen. All my poems were really about words. Like Pablo Neruda, I wanted to hold them in my fist, rub against them, twist them through my hair. I wanted to roll them on my tongue, bite and chew them, gobble them up.

Mrs. Stohl loved everything I wrote. And when school ended in June, she presented me—our class poet laureate, as she put it—with a book. Inexplicably, it was a biography of Betsy Ross. It didn't matter: I had become a word person. Thirty-five years later, I'm still one.

Mrs. Stohl, wherever you are: Thank you.—*Mary Roher-Dann*

"YOU MAY SIT DOWN, MR. PRESIDENT"

A tall, regal lover of books, grammar, and discipline, Sister Helen Bernard was a legendary figure in the Catholic high school where I served out my sentence. Pity the student who entered her classroom unprepared—Sister Helen would find you out and make you pay, usually by parading your ineptitude in front of your peers.

On the day I was elected president of my freshman class, Sister Helen let me have it. We were sitting in fourth-period English when the returns came in over the public-address system. After a smattering of polite applause, Sister Helen, who bore an uncanny resemblance to John Houseman, the actor who played a frosty and demanding law professor in the TV series *The Paper Chase*, ordered me to stand.

"Mr. Markey," she said, "please tell the class where you and I first met."

I was sunk. My backyard abutted a thirty-acre patch of suburban woods not far from the school; on the far side lay the convent where the nuns lived. As a kid I spent hours playing in those woods, occasionally straying onto the convent grounds, which felt like a secret paradise: flowering trees, blackberry bushes, secluded courtyards. In one of my explorations, when I was twelve, I noticed the irregular brickwork of the convent walls, every third brick jutting out a few inches all the way up to the wide, flat roof. The allure was irresistible.

"Sister," I mumbled in front of the tittering class, "I was on the convent roof." Leave it at that, I figured, and maybe everybody would think I had been putting down shingles or performing some equally arcane and worthy labor. Sister Helen would have none of it.

"And what were you doing on the convent roof?"

In fact, I'd been doing nothing at all. I had no ulterior motives; I wasn't trying to catch a glimpse of the nuns in their nighties or with their supposedly shaved heads exposed. I climbed onto the roof simply because I could, and about half a second later Sister Helen barreled onto the lawn and commanded me to come down, come down at once, young man. I was sure I would go to jail. Sister took me inside, into the forbidden city itself, and handed me over to a group of stone-faced colleagues. She then withdrew, whereupon the other nuns gave me a drink of water, called my parents, and told me never to let them catch me messing around on their property again. Case closed—or so I'd thought.

"I climbed up to see what was there," I lamely offered.

"You were trespassing," Sister Helen boomed.

"I was trespassing, Sister."

"You may sit down, Mr. President."

I did, quickly.

Surely Sister Helen meant to give me a short lesson in humility. "You may be president, but you're also an unauthorized roof-climber, so don't let this fleeting accomplishment swell your head." This I understood and accepted at once. It took me longer to appreciate a second, more subtle point that I think she also intended. Aptly literary, it concerned the nature of perception, an appearances vs. reality sort of thing. What you see, she was saying (trotting me out as Exhibit A), is not necessarily what you get. There is always more than meets the eye.

Sister Helen provided an indispensable lesson that day, one with many practical, as well as literary, applications. For instance, I recall it every election year when, chuckling knowingly, I pull the lever for some Washington pol whose hot-shot swagger conceals, at the very least, an earlier incarnation as a twelve-year-old goofball.—*Kevin Markey*

FOUL IS FAIR AND FAIR IS FOUL

Mrs. Hill stood on a little school desk the first day of tenth-grade English, shouting the opening lines of *Macbeth* in a nasal, squeaky voice. Her hair was jet-black and newly permed, the tight spirals framing her stark white face. She played all three witches at once; despite her slight appearance, she could belt out convincing Shakespearean lines.

The students stared up at this strange figure not in awe, but in a combination of embarrassment and amusement. For most of my classmates, this demonstration failed to edge out the infinitely more important thoughts swimming through their heads: "Who will I take to the dance?" "How can I get him to notice me?" Or "How can I make my nose bleed so I'll have an excuse to escape from this class?"

Mrs. Hill was a font of knowledge. She was a professor at New York University at night, and her educational background far surpassed that of any of her colleagues at Livingston High School. She truly believed in the art of teaching, in galvanizing young minds to think beyond the obvious and the superficial. "I refuse to spoon-feed you in this class," she insisted. "There will be absolutely no regurgitated learning in here. You must think and analyze, not simply repeat and forget."

True to her word, Mrs. Hill did not simply hand out dittos or test our memorization skills. She wanted us to find our own meaning by thinking about literature analytically. To my classmates, this seemed outrageous. They were very good at memorizing and spitting back information on tests. They were not interested in expanding their minds, especially if it meant changing their habits.

I decided to take part in Mrs. Hill's teaching experiment, and soon found that despite her eccentricities, she was loving, devoted, and fair; she quickly took a compassionate interest in me personally. I suffered at the time with several autoimmune diseases, including arthritis and ulcerative colitis. My illnesses often prevented me from attending class, so Mrs. Hill set aside special tutoring sessions for me on days when I was feeling well enough to learn. Her extraordinary devotion pushed me to new academic heights. She taught me how to write a funnel-shaped introductory paragraph, beginning with a broad statement and ending with a tightly focused thesis. And even though many of my papers came back with more red marks than words I had written, Mrs. Hill succeeded in teaching me the writing skills I would rely on all through college.

In truth, though, these private tutoring sessions were as much to compensate for wasted class time as to make up for what I'd lost due to ill health. My classmates could not bear to fritter away their time learning, and so they thought of endless ways to avoid completing assignments. Mrs. Hill did not question their integrity, choosing instead to work with the little they consented to do. She constantly came up with new incentives for working—contracts, creative exercises, rewards. One day she walked into class with a syllabus, intending to introduce us to a grownup way of organized learning, the kind we would find in college. The class immediately put this exotic idea to use. It made a high-speed jet that could stay airborne for about fifteen seconds—somewhat longer than the attention span of most of my classmates.

In our private sessions, Mrs. Hill never once complained to me about the other students' insolence and disrespect. She had too much respect for the student-teacher relationship, and to take me into her confidence would have meant crossing the line.

But everyone has a breaking point. Mrs. Hill's came just two weeks before the end of the school year. In the middle of reciting a poem, she simply stopped. In a raspy voice, she finally said, "I am a human being, whether you think so or not." At that moment, as if on cue, the bell rang, and everyone shuffled out.

I learned a great deal that year: about writing, of course, but even more about devotion and compassion, perseverance, courage, honesty, dignity in adversity, and finally, grace in failure. These were not easy lessons, but like most hard-won knowledge, they will never leave me. I still wonder what my classmates learned.—*Lori Heir*

IT'S NEVER ABOUT KINGS

When we think back on our most colorful teachers, many of us remember them as indistinguishable from the subjects or stories they loved: the geography instructor who dressed up as Christopher Columbus, the psych professor who looked like Freud, the literature teacher who acted out "The Miller's Tale." Lang is my gentleman caller or Blanche Dubois's dead husband—always outside the present moment, a character largely of my own making and still imbedded in all I do.

I. Langdon Losey. Even his name sounded like something out of Tennessee Williams. That's why the last person I expected on the first day of high school was this impeccably dressed, stooped, middle-aged, strawberry blonde with thick Groucho Marx glasses. His khaki trousers hung over his perfectly polished dress shoes, and he walked with both hands in his blazer pockets. He had a quirk of rubbing his thumb to his pinkie when he was thinking. "Play the game, play the game," he'd coach in that silence after a question. His speech was painfully slow. He was crabby and reticent and often casually cruel. On bad days, he said to us, "You wash over me like a wave." On worse days, he ignored us from behind his newspaper.

These details have ceased to matter. What does matter is that Lang was the first English teacher I knew who breathed the literature he taught. These days, as a writer and teacher myself, I make my living from words. The poetry I offer my college freshmen is as concrete as an exercise in time management. I carry a notebook everywhere to record details or snatches of dialogue until I have time to use them. But as a high school student, I had no one to tell when I was moved to tears by what I read.

Lang didn't liberate me at fourteen, although that would make a much better story. He merely tossed me a crumb. "Best in the class," he wrote on my papers, and it meant enough that I enrolled in his courses every semester. I thought Lang had dropped to Earth from Mars, and I desperately wanted to go back with him to his home planet, to a place where written words could provoke such emotion.

Looking back at a high-school teacher is rather like confronting a childhood bully when you're thirty: you try to figure out, from the vantage point of maturity, why that person exercised such power over you. I'm not quite sure how a Shakespearean actor like Lang ended up a Catholic high-school English teacher, but I do know that he stood apart from the glibness of my other teachers: the ones who knew who was dating whom and who scored the winning touchdown at Friday night's football game; those who wanted nothing more than to entertain and please us; others for whom teaching at a Catholic school was their life's work; community builders whose idea of community fit me a like a pair of saddle shoes a size too small. Lang was one of those great teachers who see students not as they are but as who they might become—a vision completely out of sync with the educational orthodoxy that held sway in my school. (In such a bland setting, Lang seemed even more eccentric.

My most enduring connection to Lang is that he sent one of my poems to the diocesan newspaper. The rule of firsts says I should clearly remember my first published piece, but I can recall only the title, which Lang gave me as a gift.

"Epiphany," he said slowly, moving his thumb to his pinkie as he held my poem in his other hand. "You know what that means?"

"Sort of," I lied. I was sixteen.

"You know the Feast of the Epiphany, of course, of course."

I so wanted to impress. "When the kings found Jesus," I regurgitated, summoning up ten years of religion class. Chances are I listed the kings in my head: Melchior, Balthazar, Caspar. Good student that I was, I may even have recited the names out loud.

"No. No. No," he said, looking at the blackboard. "More than that. A discovery. Not kings, never. It's never about kings."

All that I learned in religion class that day meant nothing. The details around me meant everything.—*Patti See*

AN AUTOCRAT, A PRANKSTER, AND AN INSPIRATION

I was the smallest child in Miss Viola Erickson's second-grade class at Maplewood School in Puyallup, Washington—so tiny I could barely see over the top of my desk in the front row, where Miss Erickson seated me on the first day of school. As her low-pitched voice boomed above me, I would struggle to get a glimpse of her feet. But all I could see was her mid-section, clothed in small-patterned fabric, which seemed to float back and forth in front of me.

"I won't pass you to third grade," Miss Erickson warned me early in the school year, "if you don't give me your dimples for Christmas." I knew I couldn't give her my dimples, but I wasn't about to say so. Although she was not a tall woman, Miss Erickson's size relative to mine confined my response to a self-conscious smile.

Miss Erickson was an autocrat in the best tradition of American elementary-ed teachers. She had exacting standards and drilled us relentlessly. But she also encouraged creativity and honest pride in our achievements. I can still recall the satisfaction I felt as I learned to write the numbers to 1,000, mastered cursive writing, and perfected the skill of answering questions with complete sentences. Whenever the high-school baseball team had a game, Miss Erickson would lead us in a rendition of "Take Me Out to the Ballgame." Her emphasis on pronunciation and rhythm helped me appreciate the stories and poems my parents read aloud at home and turned me into a lifelong lover of language.

Miss Erickson also introduced me to the joys of performing. That spring, our class put on a play. The scene was a classroom, and I was cast against type as a misbehaving pupil. Although my costume was a typical schoolgirl's cotton dress and dark-brown braids with red bows, my character exuberantly chewed gum, forbidden in real school. When the teacher in the play asked why I was chewing gum, I replied, "Mother says it makes my hair curly." As I heard the audience laugh, my stage fright dissolved. Today, as a teacher myself, I can trace the confidence I feel facing a roomful of students to that moment.

When I was ill, Miss Erickson sent me a packet of worksheets addressed to "Barbara Schonborn, in care of the chicken pox." In the accompanying letter, written in her trademark purple ink, she urged me to get better soon and told me how much everyone missed me. Getting this sort of special attention from a teacher helped alleviate the loneliness and boredom I felt as I recuperated for two long weeks in a bedroom my mother kept dim to protect my eyes.

Underneath her prim and proper exterior, Miss Erickson was also a sly and unrepentant prankster. One day, in the middle of lunch hour, the whole earth shook, and everyone in school scrambled out into the playground. After the earthquake was over—fortunately, it was a mild one—we returned to our classroom, where we discovered that our pet goldfish had spilled out of its bowl. Mischievously, Miss Erickson placed the dead fish on a paper doily and laid it on Ricky Svendsen's desk. When Miss Erickson turned her back to write on the blackboard, Ricky carried the goldfish and doily to her desk.

That afternoon, still upset from the near-calamity, I asked Miss Erickson if I could stay inside during recess. That's how I happened to be the sole witness (and unwilling coconspirator) to her revenge on

Ricky: cautioning me to remain silent, she slipped the goldfish and doily into his lunchbox. I never told Ricky who did it, but I could imagine his chagrin at finding the dead fish at home. It was a mean prank, and even now, decades later, I can't quite reconcile it with the caring adult I admired so much.

The summer I turned ten, my family moved from Washington State to California, but I continued to receive Miss Erickson's handwritten purple notes every Christmas. Years later, in 1966, when I was a young teacher on summer vacation, I visited her during a nostalgic car trip through Washington. She greeted me kindly, but by then she had little of the vitality or idiosyncratic spunk I so vividly remembered. She died of emphysema not long afterward.

Miss Erickson's lasting gift to me has been a passion for education. The first time I became fully aware of her influence was when I was a graduate student, teaching seniors who were preparing to teach elementary school. One twenty-one-year-old protested my insistence on complete sentences in their written work. As I explained that teachers were role models, and as such, must maintain high standards in written communications to students and their families, I suddenly flashed to Miss Erickson standing in front of my too-large second-grade desk. That, it dawned on me, was where I'd first seen those high standards demonstrated.—*Barbara Schonborn*

THE NATURAL

Even after all these years, when alumni from the 1950s gather at reunions, sooner or later the talk turns to Dr. Emory Quinter Hawk, economics professor extraordinaire at Methodist College in Birmingham, Alabama. Although he came late to teaching—he'd enjoyed a distinguished first career as an economist in FDR's administrations—Dr. Hawk was a natural if ever there was one.

I was half-asleep at my desk when he called the roster on the first day of our introductory economics course. "Well, Mr. Jones," he said, "there seems to be some question about your intelligence."

Indeed there was. After my father died of a heart attack while I'd watched helplessly—a terrible thing for a seventeen-year-old to witness—I had gone wild and pretty much stayed there. To pay for college, I was delivering papers from 1:00 a.m. to 4:00 a.m., seven days a week, in a desolate coal-mining area north of Birmingham. Driving sixty miles every day and drinking heavily, I was involved in all manner of mischief and staying just this side of expulsion. I seldom studied or bought my course textbooks, relying instead on the notes I haphazardly scribbled

during class, which I attended erratically.

And somehow Dr. Hawk intuited all this, right off the bat. After his opening gambit that first day, he made it clear that I was a challenge to him. Dr. Hawk, whose sharp features resembled those of the bird whose name he shared, was not going to allow me to slack my way through his course.

Our classes existed in a state of controlled pandemonium, with fascinated students learning in ways they'd never imagined they were capable of. Early on, Dr. Hawk informed us that he was a strict grader. He explained that he hadn't decided whether he was going to use the "fan" or the "step" method. The former involved holding students' tests before a fan, with the ones that fluttered farthest away getting the best grades. The latter involved throwing the tests up a flight of stairs to see which landed on the farthest steps.

Despite this capriciousness—or, more likely, because of it—he was wildly popular, and he always had a cluster of adoring students waiting outside his office. He was a great spinner of yarns in the best southern tradition. One story he loved to tell—in retrospect, I realize it was probably apocryphal—was about a ministerial student who was failing economics. One day, the young man came to Dr. Hawk with tears in his eyes, pleading for mercy. He couldn't fail the class, he said, because he

had had a dream in which the giant golden letters GPC had appeared before him. These letters, he explained, were an injunction from God to "Go Preach Christ."

Dr. Hawk claimed that he replied, "I don't doubt you at all about the letters, son. You just missed what GPC meant. What God was sayin' was 'Go Pick Cotton'." We all roared, delighted by his irreverence (an exceedingly rare and precious commodity in that part of the Deep South).

Never in my life, before or since, have I seen a teacher who had such rapport with his students. It was evident from the gleam in his eye and the grin on his lips that he enjoyed us as much as we enjoyed him. He was genuinely, if amusedly, interested in bringing out our best. And he succeeded beyond our wildest dreams.

"Now, Mr. Jones," he'd say in his signature drawl, "if you were sittin' under a dogwood tree with a pretty blonde, how would you explain the structure of the Federal Reserve System to her?"

Nearly fifty years later, my days of being under a dogwood tree with a blonde are long gone, but I can still deliver a passable explanation of the Federal Reserve System to anyone game enough to listen.

Veteran New Dealer that he was, Dr. Hawk made no secret of his politics. After Eisenhower was elected (he called him "Eisenhoover"), he sent sympathy cards to all the Democrats in class. He warned us to get

hunting dogs because a Republican depression was on the way. (I soon began receiving brochures by the dozens from local kennels.)

He quickly determined our political opinions and then pitted us against each other in formal debates. At the time, I was a fire-eating liberal Democrat, but I studied hard and prepared meticulously for these debates because I soon discovered that sheer passion wasn't enough. We had to get our facts straight and be able to get quickly to the root of the question. Otherwise, Dr. Hawk would let us have it.

I don't mean to imply that he picked on people, but the classroom was his stage and all his students—regardless of political persuasion—were straight men for his usually gentle, but always penetrating, wit. It wasn't until years later that I truly appreciated what a valuable learning experience he provided. In Dr. Hawk's class, I finally learned to use my mind.

Dr. Emory Quinter Hawk has been in his grave for more than forty years. But not long ago my alma mater asked alumni to vote on which three professors had exerted the most influence in the college's entire one hundred-plus years. When all the ballots were counted, there, staring slyly out from the pages of the alumni newsletter, was Dr. Hawk—one of the all-time greats.

These days, when we old-timers gather for our infrequent alumni reunions and reminisce about those golden days and starry nights of our youth, the conversation invariably turns, sooner rather than later, to Dr. Hawk. We still laugh uproariously at all the familiar anecdotes, but eventually someone always says, in a pensive tone, "You know, it's hard to explain, but after all these years, it's amazing how much of what he taught has stayed with me."

We loved him. Respected him. And in sweet memory still honor him.—*George H. Jones*

CHAPTER TEN

In the Presence of Greatness

All good students recognize it when it happens: the blessing of being taught by a teacher whose thinking is so elegant, whose method is so impeccable, that we can only sit back in mute wonder and gratitude at being allowed to witness the intricate workings of a superior mind.

Not infrequently, as it happens, these teachers are the very people who have helped mold the intellectual character of our culture. Yet not all great thinkers make great educators—and therein lies the mystery at the center of all good teaching. When greatness of thinking and of teaching are united in one person, however, the intellectual and emotional impact is often so profound as to defy logical analysis. In his reminiscence of Woodrow Wilson, Raymond D. Fosdick describes the Princeton professor and twenty-eighth President as "a scholar in action, a prophet touched by fire, with unmatched strength to persuade and move the hearts of his listeners." The poet Philip Levine remembers his mentor John Berryman as an inspirational teacher who "brought to our writing and the writing of the past such a sense of dedication and wonder that he wakened a dozen rising poets from their winter slumbers so that they might themselves dedicate their lives to poetry." The effect, in short, is not unlike a religious experience: "I thought, at the time, I'd undergone a conversion," admits William Gass, recalling here his first encounter with a messiah named Ludwig Wittgenstein.

Most of the teachers in this chapter derive their greatness primarily from their prowess as philosophers or poets or statesmen, and only secondarily for their teaching abilities. A glittering exception is Mark Van Doren, a Pulitzer-Prize winning critic, poet, and all-around man of letters, and the subject of two reminiscences here. It is truly extraordinary how much has been written about Van Doren, the teacher. Everyone, it seems, who wandered into his literature classes at Columbia University's Hamilton Hall was immediately awestruck by his gifts. Indeed, such a wondrous and rare teacher, as his former student Thomas Merton says, "honors his vocation and makes it fruitful. Not only that, but his vocation, in return, perfects and ennobles him."

MINE OWN JOHN BERRYMAN

It is impossible for me to imagine myself as the particular poet I have become—for better or for worse—without the influence of a single teacher, my one great personal mentor, and amazingly enough I found him at the head of a graduate class at the most unfashionable of writing industries, the much maligned Iowa Writers' Workshop. He was, of course, John Berryman, not yet forty years old, with one book of poems to his credit and stuck with the job of teaching poetry writing—for the first time in his life and the last.

The first time I saw Berryman he was dressed in his customary blue blazer, his arm encased in a black sling. The effect was quite dramatic. As a person and teacher, John was extraordinary. He did not play favorites: everyone who dared hand him a poem burdened with second-rate writing tasted his wrath and that meant all of us. He never appeared bored in the writing class; to the contrary, he seemed more nervous in our presence than we in his. He almost always paced as he delivered what sounded like memorized encomiums on the nature of poetry and life. He articulated very precisely, and his voice would rise in pitch with his growing excitement until it seemed that soon only dogs would be able to hear him. He tipped slightly forward as though about to lose his balance, and conducted his performance with the forefinger of his right hand. The key word here is "performance," for these were memorable meetings in which the class soon caught his excitement. All of us sensed that something significant was taking place.

A contingent of hangers-on had got in the habit of attending this class, encouraged by his predecessor. When Berryman took over the class, he immediately demanded a poem from one of this tribe. The poem expressed conventional distaste for the medical profession by dealing with the clichés of greed and indifference to suffering. John shook his head violently. "No, no," he said, "it's not that it's not poetry. I wasn't expecting poetry. It's that it's not true, absolutely untrue, unobserved, the cheapest twaddle." Then he began a long monologue in which he described the efforts of a team of doctors to save the life of a friend of his, how they had struggled through a long night, working feverishly. A decent poet, he said, did not play fast and loose with the facts of this world, he or she did not accept television's notion of reality. I had never before observed such enormous cannons fired upon such a tiny target. The writer left the room in shock, and those of us who had doubts about our work—I would guess all of us—left the room shaken.

The next Monday, Berryman had moved the class to a smaller and more intimate room containing one large seminar table around which we all sat. He was in an antic mood, bubbling with enthusiasm and delighted with our presence. He knew something we did not know: All but the hard-core masochists had dropped, leaving him with only the lucky thirteen. "We are down to the serious ones," he announced, and seemed pleased with the situation; he never again turned his powerful weapons on such tiny life rafts.

The key to Berryman's success as a teacher was his seriousness. This was the spring of the Army-McCarthy hearings, the greatest television soap opera before the discovery of Watergate. John, as an addicted reader of *The New York Times*, once began a class by holding up the front page so the class might see the latest revelation in the ongoing drama. "These fools will rule for a while and be replaced by other fools and crooks. This," and he opened a volume of Keats to the "Ode to a Nightingale," "will be with us for as long as our language endures." These were among the darkest days of the Cold War and yet John was able to convince us—merely because he believed it so deeply—that nothing could be more important for us, for the nation, for humankind, than our becoming the finest poets we could become. And there was no doubt as to how we must begin to accomplish the task; we must become familiar with the best that had been written, we must feel it in our pulse.

No doubt his amazing gift for ribaldry allowed him to devastate our poems without crushing our spirits, that and the recognition on his part that he too could write very badly at times. He made it clear to us from the outset that he had often failed as a poet and for a variety of reasons: lack of talent, pure laziness, and stupid choices. "There are so many ways to ruin a poem," he said, "it's quite amazing good ones ever get written."

One class began with a demonstration from the front page of the newspaper. "Allow me to demonstrate a fundamental principle of the use of language, which is simply this: if you do not master it, it will master you. Allow me to quote Senator McCarthy speaking of his two cronies, Cohn and Shine." Roy Cohn and David Shine were two assistants—investigators he called them—of the senator for whom he had gained extraordinary privileges which allowed Shine, for example, an ordinary enlisted man in the army, to avoid any of the more onerous or dangerous work of a soldier. "The senator said the following: 'I stand behind them to the hilt.' We now know what Mr. McCarthy thinks we do not know, that he is about to stab them in the back, abandon them both as political liabilities." John was of course correct; within a few days the deed was done. "Because he is an habitual liar, Mr. McCarthy has blinded himself to the ability of language to reveal us even when we're taking pains not to be revealed. Exactly the same thing holds true with poetic form; if we do not control it, it will control us."

What became increasingly clear as the weeks passed was that although John was willing on occasion to socialize with us, he was not one of us; he was the teacher and we were the students. He had not the least doubt about his identity, and he was always willing to take the heat, to be disliked if need be. In private he once remarked to me that teaching something as difficult as poetry writing was not a popularity contest. "Even a class as remarkable as this one," he said, "will produce terrible poems, and I am the one who is obliged to say so." He sensed that the students had themselves developed a wonderful fellowship and took joy when any one of them produced something fine.

This fellowship was a delicate and lovely thing, a quality that always distinguishes the best creative-writing classes. We were learning how much farther we could go together than we could singly, alone, unknown, unread, in an America that had never much cared for poetry.

And in spite of John's willingness to be disliked, he clearly was not disliked. Of course he was a marvelous companion, and on those evenings he sought company we were all eager to supply it, but we never forgot that, come Monday afternoon, the camaraderie would be forgotten and he would get to the serious business of evaluating and if need be decimating poems.

As the years pass, his voice remains with me, its haunting and unique cadences sounding in my ear, most often when I reread my own work. I can still hear him saying, "Levine, this will never do," as he rouses me again and again from my self-satisfaction and lethargy to attack a poem and attack again until I make it the best poem I am capable of. His voice is there too when I teach, urging me to say the truth no matter how painful a situation I may create, to say it with precision and in good spirits, never in rancor, and always to remember Blake's words (a couplet John loved to quote): "A truth that's told with bad intent / Beats all the lies you can invent." For all my teaching years, now over thirty, he has been a model for me. No matter what you hear or read about his drinking, his madness, his unreliability as a person, I am here to tell you that in the winter and spring of 1954, living in isolation and loneliness in one of the bleakest towns of our difficult Midwest, John Berryman never failed his obligations as a teacher. I don't mean merely that he met every class and stayed awake, I mean that he brought to our writing and the writing of the past such a sense of dedication and wonder that he wakened a dozen rising poets from their winter slumbers so that they might themselves dedicate their lives to poetry. He was the most brilliant, intense, articulate man I've ever met, at times even the kindest and most gentle, and for some reason he brought to our writing a depth of insight and care we did not know existed. At a time when he was struggling with his own self-doubts and failings, he awakened us to our singular gifts as people and writers. He gave all he had to us and asked no special thanks. He did it for the love of poetry.

—*Philip Levine*

A SECRET SOCIETY OF PHILOSOPHERS

During my second year at Brandeis, I had picked up *Eros and Civilization* by Herbert Marcuse and had struggled with it from beginning to end. That year he was teaching at the Sorbonne. When I arrived in Paris the following year, he was already back at Brandeis, but people were still raving about his fantastic courses. When I returned to Brandeis, the first semester of my senior year was so crowded with required French courses that I could not officially enroll in Marcuse's lecture series on European political thought since the French Revolution. Nevertheless, I attended each session, rushing in to capture a seat in the front of the hall. Arranged around the room on progressively high levels, the desks were in the style of the UN General Assembly room. When Marcuse walked onto the platform, situated at the lowest level of the hall, his presence dominated everything. There was something imposing about him which evoked total silence and attention when he appeared, without his having to pronounce a single word. The students had a rare respect for him. Their concentration was not only total during the entire hour as he paced back and forth while he lectured, but if at the sound of the bell Marcuse had not finished, the rattling of papers would not begin until he had formally closed the lecture.

One day, shortly after the semester began, I mustered up enough courage to put in a request for an interview with Marcuse. I had decided to ask him to help me draw up a bibliography on basic works in philosophy. Having assumed I would have to wait for weeks to see him, I was surprised when I was told he would be free that very afternoon.

From afar, Marcuse seemed unapproachable. I imagine the combination of his stature, his white hair, the heavy accent, his extraordinary air of confidence, and his wealth of knowledge made him seem ageless and the epitome of a philosopher. Up close, he was a man with inquisitive sparkling eyes and a fresh, very down-to-earth smile.

Trying to explain my reasons for the appointment, I told him that I intended to study philosophy in graduate school, perhaps at the university in Frankfurt, but that my independent reading in philosophy had been unsystematic—without regard for any national or historical relations. What I wanted from him—if it was not too much of an imposition—was a list of works in the sequence in which I ought to read them. And if he gave me permission, I wanted to enroll in his graduate seminar on Kant's *Critique of Pure Reason*.

"Do you really want to study philosophy?" Professor Marcuse asked, slowly and placing emphasis on each word. He made it sound so serious and so profound—like an initiation into some secret society which, once you join, you can never leave. I was afraid that a mere "yes" would ring hollow and inane.

"At least, I want to see if I am able," was about the only thing I could think of to answer.

"Then you should begin with the Pre-Socratics, then Plato and Aristotle. Come back again next week and we will discuss the Pre-Socratics."

I had no idea that my little request would develop into stimulating weekly discussions on the philosophers he suggested, discussions which gave me a far more exciting and vivid picture of the history of philosophy than would have emerged from a dry introduction-to-philosophy course.—*Angela Davis*

A PROPHET TOUCHED BY FIRE

I heard Lloyd George at the top of his form in the budget debates in the House of Commons in 1909. I heard Asquith and Lord Balfour on several occasions, and William J. Bryan as well, particularly in his later days. I heard Senator Beveridge and other great speakers of their time. In sheer ability and power, it seems to me that Woodrow Wilson towered above them all. He was a scholar in action, a prophet touched by fire, with unmatched strength to persuade and move the hearts of his listeners.

This ability to express himself in cogent, vivid phrase was one of the reasons, I suspect, why he was so outstanding as a teacher. I have never seen his equal in a classroom, whether the room was a lecture hall, crowded with four or five hundred students, or a curtained-off cubicle for a hastily improvised seminar, or, best of all, his study in Prospect, the President's home in Princeton, with three or four of us asking him questions. More than any other man I have ever met, he seemed to personify the dignity and power of ideas. He made the life of the intellect attractive. It was through him that we became aware of our inheritance of the rational tradition that was born in ancient Greece—a tradition of candid and fearless thinking about the great questions of liberty and government, of freedom and control.

Wilson's regular courses were in jurisprudence and in constitutional government, given on the top floor of old Dickinson Hall to a class of perhaps five hundred students. He always started his lectures with the salutation: "Good morning, gentlemen." He generally had a page of notes on the lectern in front of him—notes written in shorthand, for he was a master of shorthand—but he seldom appeared to refer to them. Occasionally he would interrupt his lecture with the remark: "Now gentlemen, I suggest you take this down," and he would dictate slowly and succinctly some idea he had been developing.

I can still see his strong, long-jawed, animated face and hear the cadences of his amazing extempory eloquence. No matter how he began them, his sentences always came out in perfect form. Occasionally when he plunged headlong into an involved sentence structure, I would think to myself: "There's a sentence he can't extricate himself from," but I was always wrong. Not only were his sentences works of art, but his argument was presented with a convincing skill and an intellectual brilliance which held his students spellbound, so that frequently they broke into applause and stamped their feet at the end of his lectures—an almost unheard-of occurrence in the conservative traditions of Princeton.

It was not his regular lectures, however, but in his informal and sometimes casual contacts with his students that he made his deepest impressions—his occasional talks at Whig Hall, one of the two debating societies on the campus; the more or less informal seminars at which his attendance, because of his administrative duties, was necessarily irregular; and particularly the occasional meetings with small groups in his own home. On some of these evenings his brother-in-law, Stockton Axson, read Browning or Wordsworth to us. Wilson was fond of poetry and read it himself with great effect.

I recall on one occasion—just what it was I don't remember—the dramatic earnestness with which he described the Covenanter movement in Scotland in 1638—the forbidding Sunday morning in Greyfriars churchyard, under the shadow of Edinburgh Castle, when the grim and determined citizens signed their names to the Covenant on a flat tombstone just outside the door. Years later, because I had never forgotten his description of it, I went to the churchyard to see for myself the setting and background of the incident. To Wilson it was one of the outstanding events in the long struggle for liberty. It was here that freedom of conscience took root; this was a stepping stone by which the past made its way into a future of wider justice. We who had the privilege of listening to him when he was in this kind of mood always came away feeling that we had been in the presence of someone upon whom had fallen the mantle of the old prophets of liberty.—*Raymond B. Fosdick (1883–1972)*

A MEMORY OF A MASTER

Professor Gregory Vlastos had completed his paper on Reinhold Niebuhr. The paper was excellent but the discussion had swallowed itself as such things sometimes do (one was only inclined to cough), and even the effort to be brilliant at someone's expense seemed no longer worth the trouble, when the funny, shabby man began speaking. At least he seemed shabby, though I remember giving him small notice at first. Old, unsteady, queerly dressed, out of date, uncomfortable in space, he struck me as some atheistical, vegetarian nut who'd somehow found his way to this meeting of the Cornell Philosophy Club and would, at any moment, heatedly, endlessly, support and denounce with wild irrelevance whatever simple, single thought was burning him up. But he'd been silent and I'd forgotten about him. Now he spoke, clearly yet haltingly, with intolerable slowness, with a kind of deep stammer involving not mere sounds or words but yards of discourse, long swatches of inference; and since these sentence lengths, though delivered forcefully, indeed with an intensity which was as extraordinary as it was quiet, were always cut short suddenly—in midphrase, maddeningly incomplete—and then begun again, what you heard was something like a great pianist at practice: not a piece of music, but the very acts which went into making that performance.

Thus in this sudden, silly way began what was to be the most important intellectual experience of my life, yet it was an experience almost wholly without content, for it was very plainly not just what the old man said that was so moving, it was almost entirely the way in which he said it, the total naked absorption of the mind in its problem, the tried-out words suspended for inspection, the unceasingly pitiless evaluation they were given, the temporarily triumphant going forward, the doubt, despair, the cruel recognition of failure, the glorious giving of solutions by something from somewhere, the insistent rebeginning, as though no one, not even the speaker, had ever been there. Without cant, without jargon, and in terms of examples, this abstract mind went concretely forward; and is it any wonder that he felt impatient with twaddle and any emphasis on showy finish, with glibness, with quickness, with polish and shine, with all propositions whose hems were carefully the right length, with all those philosophies which lean on one another, like one in a stupor leans against a bar? No wonder he was so jealous of his thoughts, no wonder he so entirely hated those who seized on his results without the necessary labors, as one might who'd sacrificed himself for summits only to await there the handclasps of those who had alighted from helicopters he'd designed; for he felt philosophy to be an activity, this very activity he was entering on before us, exactly as Valéry had felt concerning the creation of poetry, where every word allowed to remain in a line represented a series of acts of the poet, of proposals and withdrawals which, in agony, at last, issued in this one, and how no one word was final, how the work was never over, never done, but only, in grief, abandoned as it sometimes had to be, and so, in the manner of the poet, each line of thought was a fresh line, each old problem no older than the sonnet, invented today, to be conquered again for the first time, never mind if you've written a thousand; and a murmur ran round the seminar table, heads turned toward Malcolm, his student, who'd brought him, but I don't know for how many this movement was, as it was for me, a murmur, a movement, of recognition.

I was also amused. Malcolm's mannerisms were like his master's, and nearby sat Nelson, one of Malcolm's students, whose own mannerisms, in that moment, seemed to me but one more remove from the Form. The three men had fashioned, whether through affinity or influence, a perfect Platonic ladder.

Wittgenstein spoke very briefly, then. He produced an example to untie the discussion. A few weeks later he met with us, the graduate students there in philosophy, for two two-hour sessions. Monologues they were really, on the problems of knowledge and certainty, but since it was his habit merely to appear—to appear and await a question—it was we who had to supply the topics, and for that delicate mission one of us was carefully briefed. G. E. Moore had once asked, staring, I suppose, at the end of his arm (and with what emotion: anguish? anxiety? anger? despair?): How do I know that this is a hand? and it was thought that the opening question might properly, safely, touch on that. Not all of us were primed, though, and before anyone realized what was happening a strange, unforeseen and uncalculated question had rolled down the table toward the master. Aristotle? Had it to do with Aristotle? And Wittgenstein's face fell like a crumpled wad of paper into his palms. Silence. Aristotle. We were lost. He would leave. In a moment, he would rise and shuffle out, pained and affronted. Then Paul Ziff put his question—ours—for it was he who had been the student appointed; and after a terrible empty moment, Wittgenstein's head came up, and he began.

I thought, at the time, I'd undergone a conversion, but what I'd received, I realize now, was a philosophy shown, not a philosophy argued. Wittgenstein had uttered what he felt could be uttered (and it was very important), but what he had displayed could only be felt and seen—a method, and the moral and esthetic passion of a mind in love. How pale seems Sartre's engagement against the deep and fiery colors of that purely saintly involvement.—*William H. Gass*

LESSONS IN MANHOOD

I was one of the last of the lucky ones, the students who had the opportunity to study with the poet, playwright, novelist, film critic, and literary scholar Mark Van Doren.

My good fortune came at the opening of the spring term of my sophomore year at Columbia University. It was 1959, and I was in the snack-bar buying lunch when a classmate asked me if I was going to take any courses with Van Doren. "Who's Van Doren?" I asked.

"He's some old guy who's retiring at the end of the term," my classmate replied. "A famous writer. He's teaching in Hamilton at one."

I wandered over to Hamilton Hall and found the classroom on the second floor. It was one of those big amphitheater-like rooms with seats in rising tiers like a movie house. I sat way up in back. Van Doren came in promptly at one and lectured for a little less than an hour. Discussing Homer's *Odyssey*, the first book of the term, he spoke in almost intimate way about its protagonist, as if he knew the man personally. He openly identified with him to us, pointing out that Odysseus is a mature man, aging, missing his family, trying to find his way home to Ithaca after the Trojan wars. He described what Odysseus probably looked like, what he felt. Clearly Van Doren had a longstanding relationship with Homer's hero and was sharing it with us now. No one raised a hand to ask a question. We were all mesmerized.

A bell rang in the hall and everyone filed out. I sat in my seat in the back row and made an instant decision: I was going to become Mark Van Doren. Setting out to do just that, I went to the registrar's office and rearranged my entire schedule so I could take all of Van Doren's undergrad courses and audit his graduate ones. I bought expensive leather-bound notebooks—specially made in Germany for music composition—in which to record his words.

I sat in the front row of all of his classes, writing down everything he said on pads of notepaper and later transcribing them into my German notebooks. (Those notebooks still have a place of honor on my bookshelves.) I stood around his desk after class, memorizing his answers to students' questions. I followed him back to his office. Once he turned and said, "Mr. Absher, is there something you want to ask me?"

"No," I said. I was happy merely to shadow him like a junior-grade *doppelgänger*. I found out where he lived in Greenwich Village, and I would take friends to see his brownstone, pointing up and saying, "That's where Mark Van Doren lives." I haunted the used bookshops on Book Row and bought everything he'd written that I could find: novels, plays, collections of radio talks, books of poetry, books on literature. His wife, Dorothy, was also a novelist and I bought her books, too.

Once I followed him home on the subway as he rode downtown with his wife. He saw me and nodded. Lord knows what he made of this weird undergraduate who seemed to turn up everywhere he went. I didn't care. I was out to become the man, so I needed to absorb him pure and simple. Is this what stalkers do? I have no idea. I preferred to think of myself as a kind of Boswell to his Samuel Johnson. As corny as it may sound, I was always interested in wisdom. My girlfriend even got me a subscription to the magazine *Wisdom*. Just a kid (and yes, a college sophomore is still a kid), I sought it relentlessly—in books, in church, at school. I majored in philosophy because I still thought philosophy was about finding it. I was smitten with Van Doren because I thought he possessed it. He was a kind of man I had never encountered before. He was the only grown man, after my father, that I ever felt adoration for.

Like my father, he dressed in conservative suits and was a supremely respectable man. Yet here he was, speaking openly and with unguarded emotion about poetry, about literature, about his feelings for the world. It was unlike any masculine behavior I had ever witnessed. And he talked about that, too. "There is nothing more boring than an all-male man, or for that matter an all-female woman," he said. "We have in all of us male and female sides." Today such sentiment is New Age stock-in-trade, but back in 1959, to a Texas kid raised among men who made their livings either in ranching or the oil business, this was revolutionary, even shocking, news.

Looking back on him now, myself a man of sixty who has published several books of poetry and essays and been a teacher of literature and creative writing for thirty-odd years, I realize that Van Doren became for me what the Greeks in Socrates' day would have called a daimon—a kind of living spirit guide. The example of his life and mind and sensibility impressed itself into the soft wax of my youthful psyche at a time when I was particularly lost and open to guidance. Or maybe I was like the Tin Man in The Wizard of Oz who needed a heart and didn't know that he already had one until someone pointed it out.

For me and for all the other lucky ones who experienced his greatness as a teacher, Mark Van Doren provided a lesson in how to be men—men with minds but also with hearts, full of feelings that arise from reading literature deeply and well.—*Thomas Absher*

A VOCATION MADE FRUITFUL

The first semester I was at Columbia, just after my twentieth birthday, in the winter of 1935, Mark Van Doren was giving part of the "English sequence" in one of those rooms in Hamilton Hall with windows looking out between the big columns on to the wired-in track on South Field. There were twelve or fifteen people with more or less unbrushed hair, most of them with glasses, lounging around.

It was a class in English literature, and it had no special bias of any kind. It was simply about what it was supposed to be about: the English literature of the eighteenth century. And in it literature was treated, not as history, not as sociology, not as economics, not as a series of case-histories in psychoanalysis but, *mirabile dictu*, simply as literature.

I thought to myself, who is this excellent man Van Doren who, being employed to teach literature, teaches just that: talks about writing and about books and poems and plays: does not get off on a tangent about the biographies of the poets or novelists: does not read into their poems a lot of subjective messages which were never there? Who is this man who does not have to take and cover up a big gulf of ignorance by teaching a lot of opinions and conjectures and useless facts that belong to some other subject? Who is this who really loves what he has to teach, and does not secretly detest all literature, and abhor poetry, while pretending to be a professor of it?

That Columbia should have in it men like this who, instead of subtly destroying all literature by burying and concealing it under a mass of irrelevancies, really purified and educated the perceptions of their students by teaching them how to read a book and how to tell a good book from a bad, genuine writing from falsity and pastiche: all this gave me a deep respect for my new university.

Mark would come into the room and, without any fuss, would start talking about whatever was to be talked about. Most of the time he asked questions. His questions were very good, and if you tried to answer them intelligently, you found yourself saying excellent things that you did not know you knew, and that you had not, in fact, known before. He had "educed" them from you by his question. His classes were literally "education"—they brought things out of you, they made your mind produce its own explicit ideas. Do not think that Mark was simply priming his students with thoughts of his own, and then making the thought stick to their minds by getting them to give it back to him as their own. Far from it. What he did have was the gift of communicating to them something of his own vital interest in things, something of his manner of approach: but the results were sometimes quite unexpected—and by that I mean good in a way that he had not anticipated, casting lights that he had not himself foreseen.

Now a man who can go for year after year without having any time to waste in flattering and cajoling his students with any kind of a fancy act, or with jokes, or with storms of temperament, or periodic tirades—whole classes spent in threats and imprecations, to disguise the fact that the professor himself has come in unprepared—one who can do without all these nonessentials both honors his vocation and makes it fruitful. Not only that, but his vocation, in return, perfects and ennobles him.—*Thomas Merton (1915–1968)*

ABOUT THE AUTHORS

LORRAINE GLENNON is the features editor of *Parents* Magazine. She was the editor-in-chief of *The 20th Century: An Illustrated History of Our Lives and Times* and *Ladies Home Journal—100 Most Important Women of the 20th Century*. She taught English composition and literature for eleven years at Baruch College. She resides in New York City.

MARY MOHLER is the managing editor of *Parents* magazine and the editor of the book *Can This Marriage Be Saved?* She taught composition and poetry at the State University of New York at Stony Brook. She lives in New York City with her three children.

ABOUT THE PRESS

Wildcat Canyon Press publishes books that embrace such subjects as friendship, spirituality, women's issues, and home and family, all with a focus on self-help and personal growth. Great care is taken to create books that inspire reflection and improve the quality of our lives. Our books invite sharing and are frequently given as gifts.

For a catalog of our publications, please write:
Wildcat Canyon Press
2716 Ninth Street, Berkeley, California 94710
Phone: (510) 848-3600 Fax: (510) 848-1326
info@wildcatcanyon.com

CREDITS

Page 64, "Kind Hearts and Cornets," from *Think Big* by Ben Carson with Cecil Murphey. Copyright © 1992 by Benjamin Carson, M.D. Used by permission of Zondervan Publishing House.

Page 99, "Sky-Blue Pink," by Mickey Clement, first appeared in *Ladies' Home Journal*.

Page 127, "More Right than Wrong," by Floyd Patterson. Used by permission of the author.

Page 132, "Pope George the First," copyright © 1999 John Fisher-Smith

Page 259, "A Secret Society of Philosophers," by Angela Davis, from *Angela Davis: An Autobiography* by Angela Davis, copyright ©1988. Used by permission of International Publishers Company, Inc.

Page 262, "A Prophet Touched by Fire," by Raymond B. Fosdick, from *Chronicle of a Generation: An Autobiography*, by Raymond B. Fosdick. Copyright ©1986 Elizabeth Miner Fosdick. Reprinted by arrangement with HarperCollins Publishers.

Page 265, "A Memory of a Master," by William H. Gass. Used by permission of the author.

Page 273, "A Vocation Made Fruitful," from *The Seven Storey Mountain* by Thomas Merton, copyright © 1948 by Harcourt, Inc., and renewed 1976 by the Trustees of The Merton Legacy Trust, reprinted by permission of the publisher.

MORE WILDCAT CANYON TITLES...

I WAS MY MOTHER'S BRIDESMAID: YOUNG ADULTS TALK ABOUT THRIVING IN A BLENDED FAMILY
Insightful stories and commentary about the challenges and triumphs of life in a blended family.
Erica Carlisle and Vanessa Carlisle
$13.95 ISBN 1-885171-34-X

LITTLE SISTERS: THE LAST BUT NOT THE LEAST
Takes a delightful look at what it is like to grow up as the youngest, shortest female in a household.
Carolyn Lieberg
$13.95 ISBN 1-885171-24-2

STILL FRIENDS: LIVING HAPPILY EVER AFTER . . . EVEN IF YOUR MARRIAGE FALLS APART
True stories of couples who have managed to keep their friendships intact after splitting up.
Barbara Quick
$12.95 ISBN 1-885171-36-6

girlfriends: INVISIBLE BONDS, ENDURING TIES
Filled with true stories of ordinary women and extraordinary friendships, girlfriends has become a gift of love among women everywhere.
Carmen Renee Berry and Tamara Traeder
$13.95 ISBN 1-885171-08-0
Also Available: Hardcover gift edition, $20.00 ISBN 1-885171-20-X

THE girlfriends KEEPSAKE BOOK: THE STORY OF OUR FRIENDSHIP
A cross between a quote book, a collection of true stories, and a journal,
this book is the perfect way to honor women friends.
Carmen Renee Berry and Tamara Traeder
$19.95 Paper over boards ISBN 1-885171-13-7

girlfriends TALK ABOUT MEN: SHARING SECRETS FOR A GREAT
RELATIONSHIP
This book shares insights from real women in real relationships—not
just from the "experts."
Carmen Renee Berry and Tamara Traeder
$14.95 ISBN 1-885171-21-8

girlfriends FOR LIFE
This follow-up to the best-selling girlfriends is an all-new collection of
stories and anecdotes about the amazing bonds of women's friendships.
Carmen Renee Berry and Tamara Traeder
$13.95 ISBN 1-885171-32-3

AUNTIES: OUR OLDER, COOLER, WISER FRIENDS
An affectionate tribute to the unique and wonderful women we call
"Auntie."
Tamara Traeder and Julienne Bennett
$12.95 ISBN 1-885171-22-6

THE COURAGE TO BE A STEPMOM: FINDING YOUR PLACE WITHOUT
LOSING YOURSELF
Hands-on advice and emotional support for stepmothers.
Sue Patton Thoele
$14.95 ISBN 1-885171-28-5

CELEBRATING FAMILY: OUR LIFELONG BONDS WITH PARENTS AND SIBLINGS
True stories about how baby boomers have recognized the flaws of their
families and come to love them as they are.
Lisa Braver Moss
$13.95 ISBN 1-885171-30-7

INDEPENDENT WOMEN: CREATING OUR LIVES, LIVING OUR VISIONS
How women value independence and relationship and are redefining
their lives to accommodate both.
Debra Sands Miller
$16.95 ISBN 1-885171-25-0

THE WORRYWART'S COMPANION: TWENTY-ONE WAYS TO SOOTHE YOURSELF
AND WORRY SMART
The perfect gift for anyone who lies awake at night worrying.
Dr. Beverly Potter
$11.95 ISBN 1-885171-15-3

Books are available at fine bookstores nationwide.

Prices subject to change without notice